BLIND DRUNK

BLIND DRUNK

LIGHT AT THE END OF THE TUNNEL FOR ANYONE
LIVING WITH A LOVED ONE'S ALCOHOL PROBLEM

ANNE MORSHEAD

BALBOA
PRESS
A DIVISION OF HAY HOUSE

Balboa Press books may be ordered through booksellers or by contacting:

Balboa Press
A Division of Hay House
1663 Liberty Drive
Bloomington, IN 47403
www.balboapress.com
1-(877) 407-4847

ISBN: 978-1-4525-6365-7 (e)
ISBN: 978-1-4525-6363-3 (sc)
ISBN: 978-1-4525-6364-0 (hc)

Library of Congress Control Number: 2012921770

Printed in the United States of America

Balboa Press rev. date: 1/15/2013

For Reina

CONTENTS

INTRODUCTION

Twelve years ago I got emotionally involved with someone who had a drinking problem. As the relationship progressed I started to focus on thinking that I could change that person; that I could control his drinking; that I could make a difference and yes, admittedly, that I could cure him of the problem. Without fully realising how, my life became consumed with managing one crisis after another, denying disappointments, trying to hide embarrassments and feeling guilty for feeling so angry even to the point of thinking it would be preferable if he was dead. I lost myself and became absent from my own life in effect just like the person who is absent when drunk and, just like the drinker under the influence of the drug ethyl alcohol, addicted to the addict. Yes, I find that difficult to say as it seems too melodramatic and totally goes against my image of myself. I am an intelligent, creative, responsible, strong and caring woman and, definitely, not one who usually accepts unacceptable behaviour from others.

But alcoholism is a family disease and affects everyone around it. Don't worry if, right now, you disagree with this statement, it took me a long time to contemplate it being a disease for the drinker never mind anyone else. Really, I didn't know any of the facts about the drug and what it does physically, mentally and spiritually. In ignorance I had the stereotypical image in my mind of dishevelled, weather beaten old men, with maybe the odd token woman, who sat on the pavement, rheumy-eyed, clutching their bottles or waving their cans, gesticulating and ranting at invisible companions. If they hadn't reached the gutter then certainly alcoholics were the sort of people who had to have a drink as soon as they woke up, went to the pub every day, slurred their speech and staggered about. The most important part of this image was my attitude towards them. I despised them, thinking them weak. I felt angry that they had let themselves get into such a state when they had a choice. They could have pulled themselves together! I know there are many people who think the same.

Maybe you recognise this description too but know it is false and you, too, are being affected by the amount someone you know, and maybe love, is drinking? Perhaps you are desperate to know what you can do about it; are stressed out and want to live a calm and peaceful life. We shall make sense of it together.

Firstly, I shall share my experience with you, my strength and hope for the future. You may recognise a lot of similar feelings and events and I always find it helps to know one is not alone. Then we'll look at the facts surrounding alcohol. Separating the myths from the facts helped me to start detaching from the problem that didn't belong to me and to focus on what was my responsibility. There are some practical tips to aid recovery but it is mostly about being willing to act in a different way ourselves whether the other person does or not.

Also, we don't have to do this alone as there are places to go and people that can help as well as good informative literature (see the appendices at the back). It's about helping to stop the flow of misery and show by experience and example that changing your own behaviour (because that is all you can do) changes your own and others' lives.

For something to change, change has to happen

When you change in a positive way you assist the whole of society. Does that sound too grandiose? Well, changing the habits of a lifetime by uncovering some of our coping mechanisms and ceasing to use these means we can live more genuinely, less defensively, subtly offering others hope that their lives can be different too.

We don't live in isolation and how we behave directly and indirectly, affects everyone. If we live contentedly (that doesn't mean we are happy all the time) and are at peace within we radiate, that rare gift, serenity.

CHAPTER 1

Experience, Strength and Hope

I remember the main hall in the Royal Berkshire hospital, England where the payphones were situated. I am standing under the Perspex canopy, that pathetic excuse for privacy, feeling naked and exposed from the waist down as the draft whistles around me. Although, maybe, that's because I am about to vocalise one of those life changing moments that by externalising it out loud, affirms reality and forever robs one of the denial of its existence. I am calling my friend and business partner, Sally, because together we run a 'gifts, novelties and jokes' shop. With the accent on the jokes part, we endlessly manage to amuse ourselves with a variety of codes, plays on words and where a sense of the ridiculous goes a long way. Consequently, when she answers, all I have to utter is DD is BB.

DD is demented Dick, my elderly father, Richard, called many things in his life but given this moniker by us ever since he muddled up his medication and was found wandering in the town late at night dressed up to go to a funeral but whose he couldn't remember. At the time I thought he and I should never have a lucid conversation again as, amongst other oddities, he wrote out nonsensical cheques for vast sums, luckily returned, and wondered why we were having a festive dinner on 25th December when, obviously, Christmas had been two weeks before. Taken to hospital he thought the ladies bringing round the tea trolley were air stewardesses and why hadn't the plane taken off for Paris? This one was easily solved by pointing out that it couldn't because of the storm outside; that part being real. Anyway you get the picture.

It had been a stressful time in general. Eighteen months previously my 'never ill' mother had collapsed after a few odd but not overly worrying symptoms and been told she had a brain tumour whereupon the doctors said it was an optimistic view to think that she had six months of her life left. She died within two. Luckily, she was able to be at home and living nearby I could help ease her distress. Strangely those two months seemed longer and the family unit of just the three of us became even more close-knit adjusting almost imperceptibly to the inevitable. As her only child, she and I were great friends and allies and after the initial shock I am quite proud of the way I handled it for both our sakes and so, really, it was a good death. But then, I have always been a 'coper'.

My father, on the other hand, appeared to be the opposite but to give him his due ever since I was a small child he had suffered extreme back pain which must have been so emotionally as well as physically debilitating. After her death I seemed to slot into her role with him depending on me a great deal. There was no question but that I should do everything possible to help ease his misery and pain except being married and having the business meant that guilt was always hovering as I shuffled the various demands. Anyway, after the wandering incident he did recover his faculties and we returned to the usual pattern. However, this time it was different. DD is BB. Demented Dick is brown bread. My Dad is dead. You have to laugh otherwise you'd cry!

That was back in 1990 and so why am I recalling it now? Because the secondary cause of death on the certificate after the medical term for a stroke was 'alcoholic liver disease'. On reading that, I remember laughing out loud and exclaiming 'that figures'! You see, my father worked in the 'booze trade'. A chartered accountant, he had started in a well known brewing company, graduated to management, and ended up in charge of the wines & spirits importing subsidiary which naturally involved imbibing, quite a few foreign tasting trips, plus a lot of freebie corporate entertainment mainly associated with the horse racing industry. There were cocktail parties and 'Pimms' on the lawn in the summertime as my parents were social drinkers of the gin & tonic brigade. They usually had a drink before dinner, well, my father had more than one whiskey and of course home measures were at least a pub double but, even though Dad was a wine merchant, they only had a glass of wine on Saturday and Sunday lunchtimes: bottles of very good claret that he had 'liberated' from the business because the label was upside down or it was an end of line product. In other words, a perk of the job! If they entertained, which was infrequent, there would be the whole works: aperitifs, wine and liqueurs. I never knew my paternal grandparents but as

3

my grandfather had been in the merchant navy it would have been odd if he had not been a drinker. My mother's parents lived close by and were genteel folk; their idea of drinking being occasionally to have a small sherry or vermouth or when celebrating a special occasion. I still have the glasses they used and by today's standards they are incredibly small–I've seen larger shot glasses!

The question I have to ask myself is: was my father an alcoholic? Can you have alcoholic liver disease and not be one? Then before contemplating the answers more questions come pouring out: what is an alcoholic? I drink and so am I one? How do you know?

Alcoholism is a family disease and children who have one or both parents suffering as a result of an addiction to alcohol have a 50% chance of becoming or marrying an alcoholic. If it is a family disease what are the effects? And would that explain why I behave in a certain way? What can I do about any of it?

This brings me to the reason for writing this book. By imparting my personal story I show conscious first-hand experience of the effects and through the courage to change, make that the necessity to change my life, I have gained knowledge of the healthy way forward.

Being familiar with drinking, drinkers and hangovers I thought I understood the effects of consuming alcohol. Boy, was I wrong? When I met the man I am with now I didn't know he was an alcoholic and over the next five years I changed into someone I didn't recognise, someone my friends started not to recognise. I became physically ill, certainly emotionally distraught and I am forced to admit now that my mental capabilities were suspect as well on many occasions. A certain colourless, clear spirit rotted my spirit in such a subtle way that I was in its thrall as much as he was and as much as he denied he had a problem so I steadfastly said to myself and the world that I was fine and okay and coping. He had become addicted to ethyl alcohol and I had become addicted to solving his problem or at the very least controlling it and sorting him out instead of myself.

Now some of you may already see yourselves in this situation and others may read it objectively as just another's story that has no belonging for you. By the end you may change your minds. And so how did I get myself into this mess? Me, a boarding school educated gal from the Home Counties in England. Who knows? Except I do know and even at the time I had a pretty good idea what I was doing. I'm afraid I have to go back in time again to go forward–a little like our tentative journey through life itself.

I told you I was married, well, I got divorced. Six months after my dad died my husband said he didn't want the relationship to continue. As far as I recall, after seven years of marriage that's exactly how he put it. Okay, things hadn't been going well at all and I was unhappy apart from being in an orphaned state grieving the loss of both parents but even so, it was a big shock. Actually we had never got on that well living together as our individual version of lifestyle was polls apart. When I asked if there was someone else he told me he would never leave me for another he just couldn't hack it any more. We even had counselling but our agendas were opposite: I wanted to work at the marriage and he wanted to separate amicably. It took an agonising year before we parted and I moved into a lovely old cottage and lived calmly, content mostly though often lonely, with my two canine companions (luckily we had no children to destroy too) and without feeling guilty for having things the way I liked them.

In hindsight I was naive hoping that after a while apart we could get to know one another again, change and start afresh. Then a 'friend' told me that of course there was someone else and I worked out the affair must have begun sometime between mum dying and my father's death. Cheers! Plus naturally everyone else had always known and never said. How I hate that and even now on recollection I feel a fool. Back then I alternated between pure rage, thinking it was all his fault (what a bastard, how dare he?) and wanting to stab him repeatedly, to weeping copiously thinking it was all mine, knowing I must be such a bad person and so un-loveable that he didn't want me anymore. Suffice to say it was a desperate time and probably all of seven years before I truly didn't mind anymore. Oh, and I turned 40 during all this—talk about a mid-life crisis!

Psychologically, it can be said that at that age I was chronologically at a natural point to become introspective and look at what I was doing in life and why I was doing it. I knew the breakdown of the marriage wasn't just my husband's fault. In an intimate relationship or any interaction for that matter difficulties always involve both people. It may only be the tone of voice in one not the words they say that provokes a reaction in the other; equally it may be the absence of something; body language too plays a large part and once we get into defensive behaviour communication can spiral downwards quickly towards resentment and isolation. I brought my insecurities to the marriage as he must have done and admittedly, I was difficult to live with. My way of coping in general is to be independent, perhaps compulsively so, and 'in charge' of any situation. Looked at negatively, that means being controlling; the 'head mistress' type though positively I am a good organiser, responsible, and trustworthy—a 'brick'. Someone else either feels safe or that they are banging their head against the proverbial wall!

Whatever was about to happen next in life, I didn't want to make the same mistake again and felt so wretched there was no option but to learn how to change. Someone I respect told me she believed I would benefit from having psychotherapy but also make a good therapist since I possessed an innate ability to incite others to change. A dangerous comment for someone who likes to feel in charge! I guess all these years later, finally, I understand that the most encouraging and genuine way to do so is to scrutinise my behaviour, adapt it and live a different example. Breaking the pattern of the past gives permission to others by showing safety in risking change. Back then it was good timing since most of us usually only change from a point of pain. Well, when things are reasonably okay, we don't rock the boat do we? The temptation is to forget the horrible times and hope they won't come back. Ha, ha!

And so, I spent quite some time having psychotherapy. Even now there still seems to be a stigma attached to therapy but starting on that road was one of the best things I have ever done and I shall be eternally grateful to my ex-husband for having the courage to make the break. He is still with the same lady who is much better suited to him, the old hippy he aspires to be. We are friends now, now that I have no pressing need for him to be different and since he has come to realise and put in place some of the principles I so vehemently championed. Plus, we still have a shared history which will always make him a part of my family.

Crucially, without his actions I doubt very much if I should ever have moved to live in Ireland. Though I am still searching for any long lost ancestors I don't know of any Irish connection and so, why did I? The short answer is because I could, with no dependants, being self-employed and in effect free and single if not young! I had sold the shop as Sally had left to get married and moved away from the area; it wasn't the same without her. I say 'sold' but really passed it on to my assistant as there had been a recession and I had taken my eye off the ball, neglecting the business or rather just not paying enough attention. It had become a womb like haven from death and destruction; somewhere to go where I belonged and was in control: security. Sally's father had died also in this period and looking back I'm sure neither of us were that jolly in a joke shop which was quite risqué at the time selling items for hen & stag parties, 40th & 50th birthdays, lots of office parties and stocking fillers at Christmas. I suppose naturally it had become a bit stale trying to continually create excitement for the customers when the element of any humour is the initial encounter. And that's before the triple whammy of death, divorce, and downturn.

However, I had another job that couldn't have been less light-hearted having trained as a couple-counsellor with a national charitable organisation. Somewhat of a joke in itself, you might think, as I was divorced but who better to know about being in trouble and strife. I joined because, rather arrogantly, I wanted to give a more satisfactory service than I felt my husband and I had received. Although a college degree is needed now, back then if we passed their rigorous selection process they trained us in exchange for a number of voluntary counselling hours which meant that a good cross-section of society was available to assist the cross-section of society seeking help.

But this still doesn't answer the question of why Ireland although it helps my own search for clarity as to why I ended up in such a heap. Having already said I thought I knew about alcohol, by becoming a counsellor the same goes for relationships and the ability to manage affairs of the heart in the future since, what with therapy and the training, I had ironed out any possible failure. How pompous that sounds, who did I think I was?

One day a girlfriend said: "Let's go to Dublin, I've got air miles to use". Well, you know how stuff happens just at the right moment? You are in the right place at the right time in the right frame of mind: serendipity. It's an art and described as the faculty of making lucky and unexpected 'finds' by accident or maybe it's just that the gods are smiling–not only small everyday events but those that mean we are propelled forward into the next chapter if we pay attention and have the intuition at the time. Dublin was vibrant, full of music, art and theatre. Half the population of the city was under 35 years of age and the 'Celtic tiger' was beginning to roar loudly creating a feeling of excitement and expectation of possibilities previously suppressed. As they say 'the craic was good'. For me, Irish people know how to have a good time, are passionate, a race given to spontaneity with a healthy disregard for rules, well read and knowledgeable, holding an informed opinion with which they are always ready to regale anyone they come across. Despite some comforting familiar similarities to the way of life in England, Ireland was a foreign land and full of promise. Anything seemed achievable. The zeitgeist was alive and well and living in Dublin's fair city.

Returning there regularly for weekends and holidays my friend and I made forays into the countryside, bouncing along the highways and byways in an old banger, often getting lost but always ending up in the perfect spot. We did it because we could and as she had no ties either we started to plan a permanent move. I would bring my dog and rent somewhere in the mountains of County Wicklow with its woods and waterfalls having completely forgotten my childhood dream of living by a 'frothy' (as I had nicknamed any tumbling mountain stream) never imagining it would happen. Be careful what you wish for!

It turned out that we 'happened' to be in an estate agent and 'happened' to see, for sale, what can only be described as a wooden cricket pavilion half way up a mountain with a panorama to die for and a very reasonable price tag or perhaps mad money as the girl said: "Sure you wouldn't want to be living there, it's far too remote" without a hint of reverse psychology sales talk. Oh yes I would! And I do more and more each day gazing at that view and full of wonder at the light falling on a spot I'd never noticed before, even after twelve years, and listening to the water gurgle on its way down to the river running through the valley below. Granted, not everyone's cup of tea but heaven to me although back then also the auspice of a hell for which I was unprepared.

We moved over in May 2000 and I met Liam in September of that year in the local pub late at night, very late. Someone warned me against talking to him; again the wrong thing to do

it seems with me as he instantly became interesting. W
twenty minutes he was holding my hand telling me th
about his life he hadn't told anyone. Now the cynic in me chirps
up 'or so he said' but then *in vino veritas*: tongues loosened
by alcohol often inadvertently speak the truth. Out came the
story of his being engaged to an English girl from Liverpool but
on a surprise visit he had discovered her in bed with another
man; of an unhappy childhood with an alcoholic father; of
being told at age 20 by a leading American eye specialist that
he would be blind by the time he was 55 due to an incurable
retinal problem, usually hereditary. I learned later that it is
called Retinitis pigmentosa which, basically, means extreme
tunnel vision, loss of colour and no vision at night at all; bright
light and sunny days are difficult too as are evening interiors
with pools of artificial light and dark patches. Though on that
particular night I didn't have a clue he couldn't really see me
at all, never mind the drinker's hazy focus. Oh, and his mother
had had cancer the previous year, seemed to recover but was
back in hospital.

Undoubtedly there was lots of psychological stuff going on
unconsciously and don't let's forget I had consumed a lot of
wine but at about 3.45am I found myself being kissed in the
car park and promising to meet for breakfast later, though the
latter failed to stick in my mind and instead I went walking
the dog in the pouring Irish rain, doing a rather attractive
impersonation of drowned rat mixed with bag lady, only to
bump into him on my return. Not my best look! Ironically, he
had not forgotten.

From there began a full-on relationship—out of the blue or
not as the case may be. Whenever I see that advertisement for

whiskey: 'The good thing about Ireland–always pouring' I am back there that morning–what possessed me to get involved with a blind drunk much younger Irishman, one of a large family, whose life experiences could not have been further from my only child, comfortable English middle class upbringing? And that's without mentioning politics or religion!

Just the usual mid-life crisis I hear you bellow: fear of getting old, desperately hanging onto youth acting out like a twenty year old, in the pub till all hours. Or maybe the influence of the media at the start of the new century: a new millennium, a new life? But it fascinates me why people get together as well as the timing too. Most of us are still attracted to, in the other, the part of us that we have shoved down into our unconscious through fear of the consequences of displaying it overtly. That somehow the other person can help us be more fully ourselves, more complete. After all, we often speak of 'our other halves'.

This unlikely liaison is still going though I'm still not sure what attracted me. Certainly I felt Liam had strength of spirit, an inner resilience to a raw deal, a real desire to create a better life and change the past. I saw his potential to stand up in the world, be counted and not shy away though maybe I need to acknowledge I might be talking about myself and projecting on to him. I know I liked his spontaneity together with his willingness to trust me and show vulnerability which I definitely suppress. Perhaps the whole way of life in Ireland is my alter-ego as it feels like home. Of course, I recognise the rescuer and caretaker in me raised their ugly heads yet again what with the eyesight and the miserable childhood. However, it wasn't until a few weeks later that I realised with a jolt that we had met before back in May.

After completing the purchase of the mountainside cabin my friend and I had gone for a celebratory glass of Guinness and toasted sarnie in the same hostelry, a haven for hill-walkers, tourists and a focal point for the local community. It was early for lunch and we were the only ones there save for the barman and a bloke, seemingly asleep at the counter, who then raised his head and ordered another pint. Noticing us staring the barman volunteered the information that he had been there since the night before! Whilst my friend was outraged he was still being served I was wondering what horrible thing was going on in someone's life that meant he needed to drown his sorrows at 11.45 on a Thursday morning. Yes, that turned out to be Liam!

Did that realisation put me off? Of course not! In the beginning I didn't know how much of a drinking problem he had. At that point it wasn't denial maybe just naivety (which the dictionary defines as being foolishly credulous). But I don't believe in chance or coincidence and still think our meeting was a 'nudge' or at least ye gods saying: "we've given you this lesson before but now we'll make it so plain even you cannot fail to learn".

Another advert, this time the Irish Tourist Board, told me: 'Ireland–Live a Different Life' and it was so absolutely different to my existence in England. I hadn't been part of the pub culture for many years; rather it had been supper with friends putting the world to rights over a bottle of wine or restaurants to celebrate birthdays; nor was I used to the city life either. Now here I was enjoying both Dublin and the countryside, going out more, doing more–back in the swing and drinking more often. To give Liam his due he did say on our first 'date' that he'd been barred from several city pubs because of 'a little bit of bother' but since it was a different life I admit it seemed amusing and quite impressive. As he was himself: very tall, a commanding presence and brilliantly able to handle and cover up his very, very limited vision plus he seemed to like me a lot. Presuming that he drank a lot because that was how it was in Ireland as 'are you going for a pint?' usually accompanied most conversations I did begin to notice I drank more alcohol in his company than I really wanted to but put it down to the continuing holiday feeling. During the following five years all the therapy received and counselling skills attained seemed to evaporate. The better-self morphed back into the one I always feared I was: ugly, very angry, demanding, punishing and controlling.

It stands to reason that we are all the sum of our parents' parts and my encapsulated recollection of growing up is one of my father as dictator and patriarch, his way being not only right but the only sensible way and brooked no dissent. He had mood swings meaning I could never quite relax and be sure of a certain reception. Thinking back, it must have been the same for my mother who never appeared to stand up for herself, acquiescent the majority of the time. Feeling the need to step into the gap I stood up to him, fighting her battles, ending up being classed as obstinate and stubborn. My father was quite the melancholic too but to be fair, after 'slipping a disc' whilst digging in the garden when I was two, was often in bed for weeks at a time in acute pain, missing work, with my mother running up and down stairs as nursemaid. And certainly growing up I never considered the quantity of prescription drugs he took only in so far as the ponderous counting out of them at the dinner table was a source of covert amusement and exasperation all at once for my mother and me. Three's a crowd and the conspiracy was there between us as females. Not just a conspiracy but a collusion too. Mum and I colluded together without my knowing it to keep him sweet, try to make him happy, feel less pain, to not be so cross or to do the right thing. There is a dichotomy for only children in my mind which is the likelihood of being mature for their age, responsible and independent but at the same time also being quite shy and retiring, perhaps under confident.

Above all I knew I had to be independent so as to never, never fall into the abyss that was my father's dependency through pain, illness and depression on my mother and her dependency on him because of circumstance, duty and the age in which she was born. Of course there were fun times on my own with her and for us all together when he was pain free and his sense of humour shone through and where I could catch a glimpse of his former self. This is not to say I don't view my childhood very fondly, one containing much privilege, security, fun and beauty but, only slightly tongue in cheek, the result of those parts means, on the one hand, Mrs Mussolini and on the other, Florence Nightingale: a controlling caretaker! A critical parent figure and a nurturing one; perfect for those of an emotionally dependent nature like addicts.

Had Liam just been drunk I wonder whether we would have got entangled but since he was blind and drunk, disadvantaged in life, presently fearful and very anxious about his mother's illness, of course, I felt for him thinking I could ease his emotional pain. His father, who had dropped dead at the bus stop a couple of years earlier, had been a raging alcoholic with Liam spending his childhood in a constant state of apprehension and fear. He had tried to cling to his mother and she probably did her best to protect him especially as he was visually impaired even though the exact nature had been left undiagnosed. As a result my guess is that he was attracted to me as a solid, older woman who had surprisingly stayed and listened to him.

We got on well. He was charming, could be good company and, although a man of few words, had an unnerving ability to get the measure of me and others and succinctly nail the state of play in one sentence; something that attracted me needing someone strong, as I do, to challenge me and not allow me to get away with too much. Education may have left him behind but intelligence and kindness were innate. And so what exactly went so wrong?

We weren't living together; I had a separate life in Ireland and regular visits to catch up with my friends in England but more and more Liam and what state he was in became my focus. This man was emotionally damaged by his abusive childhood and with his father's sudden death had lost the opportunity, however unrealistic, of having the loving parent a child always hopes for. His mother was obviously not going to get better, she had become a mere shadow of the woman I saw in photographs but as is our nature we deny reality and she, tantalisingly, was well enough to leave hospital several times only to return. The whole family were riding the emotional rollercoaster of the protracted process of dying. Somewhere, too, acknowledged or not must have been the frustration, disappointment and isolation of living with gradual sight loss always hanging over him like the sword of Damocles. I'm telling you this to mitigate my own denial that Liam had a drink problem that went beyond heavy social imbibing and I made similar excuses to others. Feelings of embarrassment and shame started to creep up on me. Of course he was trying to drown his sorrows but even when he started wetting the bed on occasions I rationalised it as a regression to an unhappy and uncertain childhood. Ha, bloody ha!

There were two incidents involving money (or maybe more). One when my purse containing a small amount of foreign currency and a key went missing. Discussing it with Liam, I blamed someone else stating that the money didn't matter but the key did and miraculously the key appeared a couple of days later. It was never mentioned again but I know it was him as was the mysterious missing 50 Euro gone from the bag he was minding while I was in the pub toilet. Toying with the idea of a pick-pocket I settled on being mistaken and must have miscalculated the amount I had in my wallet but I very rarely do that. It always amazes me how a lot of us find fault with ourselves in order to avoid having to confront an issue. Still, from then on I started to write down everything I spent, however small, and continue to this day although now I pass it off as a mental arithmetic talisman to ward off the demon dementia. Generally, Liam's financial status had not started to obsess me yet, he seemed solvent working as a labourer for good money though several Mondays and often Tuesdays too were not made into work. Originally an electrician he had been forced to abandon the trade as his eyesight deteriorated but was still refusing to acknowledge the extent of disability.

Then, never mind his, my eyes started deceiving me. He'd be up at the bar ordering a pint or round and was that a shot of whiskey or two he was having whilst waiting for the Guinness to settle? No, surely not, that's not what normal people do I must have got it wrong! Thinking back probably he was always drinking a 'Dublin pint' (a chaser poured into the stout). Certainly it would explain why he was often much more drunk than seemed feasible with my being present all the time; suddenly his mood would change not to mention the staggering, knocking into furniture and falling down but after all, I told myself, he was blind. His lack of eyesight was a big stumbling block for me! As the chauffeuse I felt mean, unable to leave him to it and go home if we were out, as it would have been unfair and immoral to tell him to go from the far pavilion in the middle of nowhere at night time since his condition meant total night blindness, but neither was I damn well going to leave my own home. Sometimes it seemed I had become the carer of a delinquent teenage rebel alternating between the nurturing parent who, when my thoughtfulness, advice and cajoling wasn't heeded, turned into the critical one who blamed, punished and criticised.

Looking back, what shifted our problem into the next gear, I say 'our' problem because he was addicted to alcohol and I was addicted to him, was that I started to confront him with it asking and expecting him to control his drinking and work towards giving up. Every morning after the night before he was compliant, remorseful and acquiescent (naturally the easiest way to get to have another drink) discussing it willingly and convincing me he would change. Again ha, bloody ha!

From then on he went underground with his habit so to speak: pretending to be sober, hiding bottles, lying more, deceiving more, in such a clever subtle way that I kept on believing him. It always sounded plausible even though the facts didn't quite add up. I stopped trusting my instincts, never being able to relax and not knowing what would be uncovered or what nasty surprise was waiting around the corner: an adrenalin overload. And so, in fight or flight mode more or less all the time, I was frequently very angry and aggressive, shouting at him like a fish wife; God knows what the neighbours heard. I felt I wasn't a nice person and it never occurred to me the feeling was similar to childhood and maybe there was a parallel with my father there. After all Dad had seemingly devolved responsibility for his actions as well by being bedridden a lot, by being emotionally absent and controlling by not complying, not being capable. Anyone who is drunk can easily reject responsibility knowing they aren't capable: the classic excuse when pissed 'Oh, sod it, I'll do it tomorrow'. Procrastination gets us off the hook.

I put things off. I put off writing another book; getting another job; catching up with old friends and promptly squashed any of my own creative ideas. Knowingly isolating myself, fearing no one would want my company, feelings of unworthiness set in and self-esteem ebbed away. I stopped accepting invitations never being sure of having enough energy to attend when the time came around and they dried up anyway because friends didn't want Liam to come too. Neither would I have. Never mind, I'm fine, I can cope, I'd tell myself and the dog. The poor dog suffered as much since animals, like children, are so susceptible to mood and atmosphere. Because of feeling increasingly insecure I shrank and shrivelled and as in a storm battened down the hatches in an attempt to control the space around me needing everything neat and tidy, in a row, all surfaces wiped clean. Not full blown obsession by any means but probably within the spectrum covered by obsessive compulsive disorder. Being resentful I would say no, enough, please don't come here if you have been drinking but either a taxi driver would deposit him at my gate or someone from the pub thinking they were doing right by us would drive him 'home'.

When Liam wasn't remorseful he could be quite aggressive towards me, never physically but emotionally very mean. And he would punch walls or repeatedly bang his head on inanimate objects thereby harming himself. He was 'upping the ante' as is the nature of the disease and my guess is he despised me for continuing to put up with him because the tape running in his head was saying: I don't deserve anyone who cares about me. He certainly did his utmost to do and say stuff that would shock me and cause enough fear for me to abandon him so he could say: of course I knew she didn't really love me as I'm worthless. He hadn't reckoned on my internal script which said: you can't change your mind, you must be stoical.

It all became so unmanageable that one night I resorted to calling the police but before they arrived he had agreed that my wonderful neighbour would take him to the nearby psychiatric hospital; apparently the *de rigueur* destination when you don't know what else to do. It's strange how somewhere that held a great stigma for me soon became a haven and a perfectly natural place to avail of their services. Basically, he dried out with the help of Valium and anti-psychotic drugs. However, as soon as he was ensconced, I collapsed and now I understand the phrase you read in period novels: 'she took to her bed' because that was me. Feeling flu-like without the symptoms, I remained prone only ingesting herbal tea and I assure you that no desire for caffeine means something is seriously wrong! It was pure and simple relief that someone else was dealing with him, no more nasty surprises or shocks, the adrenalin too suddenly not needed. It rattled me though as I'm never ill like my mother and look what happened to her.

Perhaps that phone call to the police was the beginning of recovery for me, saying out loud an inability to cope on my own. The very, very long road to recovery which, foolishly, I presumed I was further along than the stark reality. I am ashamed to say I thought: great he is sober now, understands the problem and we can go forward. Not without going back first and then forward and back many times: the dance of drug dependency. At least the problem was more overt. We could go on denying how we dealt with it but not that it existed, something that everyone else already knew. And I feel a fool reading this; anyone would ask: why is she putting herself through all this, what's in it for her? But that's addiction for you.

Life was unmanageable but I didn't know it yet. I was convinced that by sheer will power I could cure his problem or at the very least control the drinking by throwing bottles away, by pouring contents down the sink, by monitoring exactly where he was and what he was doing at all times though, thank God, no car keys to hide. Making a classic mistake, I reckoned that if Liam understood the reasons, unconsciously formed in childhood, for his feelings of hurt and anger and worked through them in counselling then he could choose to change his behaviour.

Almost a year to day of his mother's death an extremely scared Liam went into rehab. All the grief surrounding a loved parent's passing had been exacerbated, he was desperate for the pain to be taken away and I do think he wanted to and knew he had to stop drinking. That was in June 2003 with the programme running for 12 weeks. The centre was run by nuns, initially causing me to be dubious and fear too religious a slant on proceedings, but it was and still is a remarkable haven with more of a Buddhist feel to it working around four elements to each day: work, recreation, meditation and prayer. Once dried out over the course of a week there was counselling and some classes but, being a self-sufficient working farm too, everyone had to perform a job suited to them. Being able to relax for the first time in three years it was as if a weight had been lifted off my shoulders with no need to keep looking over them and the rug stayed in place under my feet. I felt positive, optimistic and hopeful that normal life could resume. On visits, contact with Liam was rewarding: he was clean and bright, forthcoming and able to be empathetic. We engaged in ordinary conversations highlighting just how dysfunctional my existence had become and I felt so sad and child-like at the excitement of being cherished even a little bit.

But as the saying goes 'this too shall pass' and a new phase of chaos was beginning meaning another two years would pass by before I finally copped on. You could say I became the drunk since there was a constant feeling of the ground moving under my feet, nothing was solid or secure and known. I upped my attempt at controlling my environment: wiping and re-wiping surfaces, checking, readjusting everything so it was in place and lined up, ship-shape and Bristol sherry fashion! Ready and waiting for whatever came but, of course, reality always caught me unawares making all efforts futile.

Needless to say Liam did not stay sober and here I wouldn't even use the word sober because at this point he had only ever been dry for a while. Recovering is all about the quality of intention and so I have to wonder whether he ever intended to? I can only say it as I perceive it to be. By then I think we both thought that someone or something outside of ourselves would help us: the waving of a magic wand I suppose. The projection of uncomfortable truths that lay within us allowed the status quo to remain. If we take back our projections and own the responsibility then we more or less have to change and change is risky and scary. Alcoholics feel so much shame and guilt more than anyone who isn't afflicted can ever realise and the only way out is to have another drink to drown the feelings and try to forget—a perpetual merry-go-round.

In my mind maybe Liam had started to lose his tolerance to alcohol (as happens when the disease becomes advanced) considering he seemed fine only to suddenly lurch and stagger about without having any opportunity to get hold of booze. However, this was the red-topped bottle phase. It is true that vodka doesn't smell on the breath to begin with but later on there is a strange whiff like the whack off dry-cleaning fluid. I never put two and two together and the quarter bottle is the perfect size for concealing about the person. Like the guilt and shame of the morning after, the lying and deceiving is part and parcel of the over-riding need to secure, or know one can secure, another top up. It's just that I don't live my life needing to deceive (except myself) and on many occasions wondered if I was going mad. At least I don't think he ever went for a snooze in the afternoon taking a hot water bottle containing something other than water!

In the end phase he was in and out of treatment centres and the psychiatric hospital and as Liam got worse so did I. Irrational fears appeared such as not being able to get on the down escalator in the shopping centre or anxiety around whether I could stop the car in time if traffic lights changed back to red together with a sudden nervousness in aeroplanes and a general persecution complex. The main and most frightening one was the heart palpitations that occurred so that even I went to the doctor and was sent for an ECG. Even though all was fine still they would happen randomly without being linked to any particular stress point. I told myself not to be pathetic especially when I realised I became physically agitated at the sight of any odd clear bottle with a red top wherever it was. Like a lot of things we only realise what was going on after we get better, when there is a contrast, and I understand now that it was panic attacks; the same as I had been so sceptical about in others. In the short term our bodies respond to fear by producing adrenalin so that we can overcome danger by fighting or fleeing (both needing a lot of energy) but during a prolonged period of stress cortisol floods the system to help us cope. A surplus of this hormone with no useful outlet means our bodies have to do anything possible to restore a balance. Still maintaining I was grand, whenever anyone asked me how I was I could only tell them how he was, regaling anyone who would listen, needing the opportunity to get things off my chest–literally!

By now Liam was experiencing blackouts and seizures. The medication prescribed by the psychiatrist that he took or didn't take or took in odd amounts can't have helped but blackouts were a new one on me–not remembering anything at all but still able to function? To remember being on a bus at 7pm and waking up in A&E at 7am with a complete gap in between, no surely not? And, on first witnessing a fit, I honestly wondered if he was having me and the hospital staff on as it seemed so contrived–one minute okay and the next writhing on the floor–necessitating yet more medical resources to be expended. Then there were the bizarre suicide attempts like hanging out of a fourth floor window over a busy thoroughfare but making sure the chosen window lined up with the open front door–risky–but he lives to tell the tale or rather lives to not really remember it. I suppose it makes a difference to fear if you can't see. I know it was true only because the ambulance drivers on a subsequent visit the following week (that time too much medication though not enough) confirmed it.

But who knows what was and was not real; by that stage I was distancing myself and forever giving ultimatums only to renege on them and enable him further. I realise this is rambling on and on and that in itself is a mirror of the whole scenario: lots of different scenes but the same old story. Worn out, feeling so embarrassed, ashamed and resentful, I was probably depressed not for the life of me knowing why he couldn't stop since he seemed to want to and was crying out for help. In fact we were in the same state: in hock to the demon drink.

What changed? Thank the Lord, I hear you say, at last! Bearing in mind that becoming addicted takes time and recovery is a process too, throughout the rehab programmes I had attended family days and lectures where the notion of 'tough love' and detachment with compassion had been voiced but I had not heard it fully. I understood it intellectually and would have been the first to counsel others to use it but the idea hadn't entered my being if you like. I couldn't yet live it. Like the well known serenity prayer I hadn't accepted the things I couldn't change, still being in the 'if I rack my brain enough by sheer will power I can come up with a way of sorting it out' mode, definitely not in a position to have the courage to change anything and so hardly the wisdom to know the difference. Two odd things in the real world changed me internally.

My car was ten years old having done well over 100,000 miles and journeys back to England were anxious ones lest a breakdown occur on the motorway creating another feeling of insecurity. I hate that situation with cars when you never know how long to carry on paying for repairs because the price of a new one is so much more but in the end you may pay as much to keep the wreck on the road. Another metaphor for my relationship with Liam and alcohol! I bought myself a new one in October 2004; it felt wonderful to be in: smart, clean, solidly safe and reliable like the feeling of being supported and cherished. I realised I actually deserved to feel safe, carefree and, dare I say it, happy. I was worth it!

Then at Easter in 2005 my dog had to be put to sleep. It was her time but, as any animal lover knows, I was inconsolable. Though, as often happens with a death, there was a feeling of relief since it had been like looking after an elderly relative with all the medication and incontinence never knowing quite when the end would come and I had needed to protect her from the chaos of the alcoholic life. I couldn't just exit a difficult situation without considering how to take her with me or where to go. Without the dog I was freer to change plans at the last minute, a big responsibility had been removed and with one less to care for there was more energy to care for myself. I had become ill as if my body was saying: 'will you ever cop on you can't cope any longer surely you don't want me to show you how bad I can get? Remember your mother's brain tumour? Don't you think that might have been years of suppressed feelings that had nowhere to go but explode in her head?'

And so, on the morning of 7th July 2005, I found myself standing in a car park in England, on my mobile to Liam, saying that I didn't want to see him or talk to him again until he had stopped drinking. I told him I cared about him, that I loved him, which I did since it wasn't him as a person it was what he had become that was intolerable. I said: "I really hope you decide to recover but I can no longer live my life like this".

After saying on many occasions before I didn't want to live like this but carrying on doing just that, what was different about this time? Such subtle shifts within the self are so very difficult to describe yet so very simple when they happen. I just felt it. I didn't think it; it wasn't the usual intellectualisation or rational, logical process of making a decision it was a whole body 'knowing'. Me, myself and I protecting one another; it wasn't hard because it was just fact, in fact it was simple and spontaneous. I stopped being co-dependent and had detached: Liam felt apart from me, physically, mentally and spiritually, separate but still close. Hearing in his voice that he was dry it was important he took on board that I cared about him and not just hear a rejection making it easier to go down the well worn 'I am worthless' path.

At the time he did say he understood and knew that I cared although now has no recollection of the phone call whereas I remember it acutely. I felt compassion at the same time realising it could be very final if he carried on drinking as he was quite likely to die if not of organ failure or suicide then by an accident through reckless, blind actions. I've always had difficulty knowing how I feel though I can always tell you what I think and years ago if asked 'how do you feel' it would have taken me a week to be able to work it out. It is easier now but still I travel up into my head at a moment's notice rather than stay with what my tummy is telling me. All I can say is that July morning my feelings and thoughts joined forces and created right action. Annoyingly, you only know when you know!

Unaware at the time of the phone call that 7th July 2005 was the day of the fateful London tube and bus bombings, on hearing the awful news perhaps it might have seemed natural to go back on what I had uttered on the principle that life is too short for estrangement and for being left alone as you never know what it round the corner but, precisely because of the bombings, that day was such a turning point for me.

Meditating on the tragedy I initially felt very insecure due to the chaos distilled into the thought of existing ordinarily and unaware one moment and then in an instant your sense of being and all around you changes irrevocably.

Then I realised the result of that chaos means there exists perfect security and no need to worry about anything as this moment is all there is, that's the only reality, and if I am okay right here, right now then that's sufficient and I have all I need. I am alone but connected with all others. I can afford to trust myself, life itself, the world. I am secure and since life is uncertain and you never know what will happen then if I am okay is this moment, I am okay for always, forever; by staying in reality and the present minute I need not be fearful. All this led to a realisation that the need to control Liam's drinking and his behaviour was a deep, deep need to keep my own fear of annihilation at bay.

When I stopped asking Liam to meet my unconscious needs he was freed to be responsible for himself. He chose to recover. I believe, since all our lives are integrated, it was no coincidence that the real start of my recovery heralded his. Of course it could have been otherwise and, very unfortunately, many problem drinkers do not choose that path in their lives but even if Liam hadn't started to recover, I did. It means I shall always have to continue to work on it.

"The intellect has little to do on the road to discovery. There comes a leap in consciousness, call it Intuition or what you will, the solution comes to you and you don't know how or why."
Albert Einstein

Okay, so you recovered, he recovered so what, I hear you say, that doesn't help me. Of course, all you probably want to hear is how *you* can stop your loved one drinking. If you can just find the right formula; try something new; say different words; persuade afresh; cajole from a new angle then you will manage it and everything will resolve itself.

You can't, it won't. Sorry. But don't throw this down in despair. There is much you *can* do and it is well known that if relatives and friends change their own behaviour then many other aspects improve too. Family life changes for the better which is of paramount importance if there are children involved.

Children suffer emotional and mental abuse if one or both parents are alcoholic and often physical and sexual abuse too. As with physical violence, the perpetrator is responsible for the abuse but the victims are responsible for their safety and as the adult you are responsible for your children's safety and security and your own. I have been incredibly lucky in that I am in charge of my own finances and have had the means to make alterations to my life, in other words not dependent on Liam or anyone else for the roof over my head or the food on the table. It is far from easy for many to escape all the difficulties of living with a loved one's drinking problem. Now I know I shall never live with 'active drinking' again but some people manage to and still maintain the happy and fulfilling life of recovery.

An alcohol related problem develops gradually, it takes time to become dependent and diseases aren't recovered from immediately. In the same way all the disappointments, resentments and the myriad of other problems you may experience are not healed overnight.

Recovery is a process but the word means that we are getting back something we've lost. We never disappeared we just mislaid ourselves and it's very important to give ourselves the benefit of the doubt, if you like, and allow ourselves the time to be able to take one step forward and sometimes two back but to always expect good to come out of our progress. A positive optimistic attitude goes a long way.

I am back to normal now–no better than that since I have more knowledge, more experience, more wisdom than before, although I'm no saint and am still making the same old mistakes but in a diluted form; now it takes less time to realise them, acknowledge them and change behaviour. Really, for me, it is still the one mistake that always starts with not minding my own business that leads to doing something for someone that he or she could do for themselves.

But we'll talk more about that later, first we need to speak about alcohol.

CHAPTER 2

First Things First

I drink. Nowadays, red wine is my tipple of choice but in the past I have tried most alcoholic drinks and consumed far too much many times. During my lifetime, in the Western world the drug ethyl alcohol has not been prohibited, in fact, it has been very actively promoted. 'Say no to drugs' but yes, yes, yes to alcohol! Everywhere we turn we are encouraged to imbibe: advertising, television, cinema, magazines. To drink is to be part of the successful, modern lifestyle we're told we must achieve not to mention the mainstay of any festivity.

In other words, the partaking of booze is very difficult to get away from. It is part and parcel of every-day life. We drink when eating out, on holiday, at sporting events, when wetting babies' heads, celebrating weddings and commiserating after deaths. We drink to relax after work; to reward achievements; to give confidence; to be part of the crowd. We drink because we don't need a reason and if we consume one then it is so easy to say 'oh, go on, let's have another'! Now, all the advertisements say 'drink sensibly'–yeah, right! Anyone can see through that one and no-one is paying the least attention because we all know what is best for ourselves and if we are lucky enough to be in recovery we have already got the message. What's the point?

The point is that most people do know about the adverse effects of alcohol and choose to deny it. The dictionary defines ethyl alcohol, also known as ethanol, as: a colourless, volatile, inflammable liquid forming the intoxicating element in wine, beer, spirits etc. The word 'intoxicating' derives from the Latin for poison. Really, we don't want to think about it in the same way that bad things happen to other people not to us. And we like them happening to other people: gawping at car crashes as we speed by so that we can feel okay because we are still in one piece and to prove the hypothesis. By doing this with alcohol we are in a double denial. Firstly, that the drug, ethanol, won't affect us as much as that other person out there since our habits are nowhere near as bad as theirs and, secondly, because it affects them it won't affect us. Of course, it is human nature to attempt to project our negative feelings and images onto other people and situations so that we don't have to feel them, deal with them or have to sit uncomfortably in our own skin. It is as difficult to stop that behaviour as much as it is to stop having 'one for the road'.

We are not concerned enough about our physical or emotional health. Why aren't we? Because drinking alcohol is enjoyable. It serves a purpose. We can have fun and lose our inhibitions. We can forget our troubles; we can drown our sorrows. The drug has become synonymous with the drink as if the contents of the glass are the alcohol even though we know there are other ingredients. Heroin addicts are more honest since they admit it is the drug they're after but we are just being sociable aren't we? Let's face it if the drug wasn't in the drink we probably wouldn't want it. The problems associated with alcohol in our society today, still underneath the surface to a great degree, are deep, long lasting and travel down the generations as does all abuse. A long time ago alcoholism might have been seen as a poor man's lot or the scourge of the working class but today, I believe, it's the so-called 'chattering' class that are most at risk and the huge consumption of wine that poses a danger and propels people towards addiction as well as the buy one get one free, 3 for the price of 2, always a 'special offer' culture.

A word here about units, particularly wine, since most people think one glass is one unit. This may have been the case many years ago when the alcohol content was much lower than today. Red wine is often 14% alcohol by volume nowadays which means 1 x 125ml glass (6 glasses in a bottle) equals 1.75 units (10.5 units per bottle). If you believe the safe amount per week for women is 14 units and for men 21 units knowing that makes quite a difference. A can of 'special brew' or strong lager contains the same amount of alcohol as a double whisky (that's measures in England & Wales). Alcohol by volume means the percentage of pure ethanol that is in the whole bottle or can or pint in other words 14% of a bottle containing three quarters of a litre is a drug. 40% of a bottle of whisky is a drug; 37.5% with vodka. If you drink 9 pints of Guinness you've drunk the equivalent of more than half of a litre bottle of whisky.

- To calculate a unit multiply the amount being drunk by the strength (ABV – alcohol by volume) and divide by 1000
- 1 x 750ml bottle of 14% red wine = 10500 divided by 1000 = 10.5 units. There are 6 x 125ml glasses in 1 bottle and therefore 1 glass = 1.75 units (note: often wine is now served in 250ml glasses meaning one glass = 3.5 units)
- 1 x 375ml bottle of lager at 5% ABV = 1.875 units
- 1 x 500ml can of cider at 4.5% ABV = 2.25 units
- 1 x measure of spirits is 35.5ml (Ireland) Most spirits are 37.5% ABV or 40% ABV and therefore a single measure = 1.33 units (37.5%) and 1.42 (40%)
- A pint is 568ml and therefore a pint of Guinness at 4.2% ABV = 2.38 units

Alcohol is a major depressant drug. It travels in the bloodstream and begins to affect the brain within 5 minutes of being swallowed. It slows down the activity of the brain but first depresses the part of the brain that controls our behaviour and our inhibitions which is why many think of it as a stimulant as it seems to increase sociability and may make the drinker noisy, over-active, often leading to aggression. When the levels in the blood increase, the drinker's movements and speech slow down; taken to extremes it can cause unconsciousness and maybe coma and even death. Alcohol increases heat loss and so the 'warm glow' one feels to begin with is heat leaving the body via the skin as peripheral circulation is increased. The drug is broken down by the liver and this vital organ can process about one unit each hour; it will start this process around 20 minutes after the first drink is consumed. Therefore to process one pint of normal strength beer will take the liver 2 hours 20 minutes and this is the same for regular drinkers as well as occasional drinkers. Taking other medication may cause alcohol to stay in the body longer.

Which of these is an effective way of sobering up: a strong cup of coffee, fresh air, making yourself sick or 'hair of the dog'? I hope it is obvious it's not 'hair of the dog'! Actually, the stimulant effect of caffeine increases the rate at which any drug is absorbed so any alcohol in the stomach will reach the bloodstream even faster and it would take huge quantities of coffee to counteract the depressant effect of alcohol on someone who is already drunk. Making yourself sick, by emptying the stomach will prevent you getting drunker but will not sober you up. The passage of time is the only way of 'sobering up'.

If only alcohol affected the liver in isolation but no, it permeates the whole body and taken regularly enough and in enough quantity takes its toll on every part of the wonderful machine working to let us live. I imagine you know this only too well but if not please consult the back of the book to get really scared. As well as a comprehensive list of what can happen you will find a list of websites and some books. Please, become informed. It is true that knowledge is power. We can't go back from knowing, even if we carry on denying for a while, and so this is the start of you getting well again.

What it an alcoholic then? Notice I say what not who because it is not who the person is but what they have become. Please, spend a few minutes contemplating this sentence:

No-one came out of the womb thinking 'I know what I want to be when I grow up–I want to be an alcoholic!'

The Marty Mann Definition is most commonly used to describe someone addicted to alcohol: "An alcoholic is someone whose drinking causes a continuing problem in any department of his or her life". The most important word is 'continuing' since a lot of us have probably regretted drinking too much at one time or another. Alcoholics Anonymous suggests this means someone who repeatedly drinks more than they intend to or want to even though they recognise from experience that they cannot control it and eventually become aware of this habit or pattern realising they are powerless to change it with any degree of certainty or permanency.

Hopefully, gone are the days when to be an alcoholic was considered to be lacking in morals or of having a vice or even of committing a sin. Although, with shame, I see that I had that sort of prejudice not that long ago together with the superior 'holier than thou' attitude. The drug has no such prejudice and makes no demands on what type of person it enthrals but picks on anyone whatever their job, beliefs, gender or age.

There's no clear line between where heavy social drinking ends and addiction to alcohol begins but anyone who drinks enough for long enough can become dependent. Being addicted means that the person has an uncontrollable urge to drink; it's a compulsion, a craving and an obsession. Again AA suggests that no one who is not afflicted can really understand this desperate drive to satisfy a need. Really we shouldn't label anyone an alcoholic as they have to decide that for themselves. The denial of having a problem usually features heavily and it's this refusal to fully acknowledge the addiction that means many never recover. This denial, having layers to it like an onion, is a defence mechanism and like all defences is a vain attempt to keep fear at bay often manifesting itself with the drinker saying: 'I can't help it, I have the alcoholic gene'. But having a particular gene is only a predisposal to contracting something not an automatic occurrence. It suggests we don't take part in what happens to us and our bodies, that we are not responsible for our actions.

Even when someone recognises they have alcohol related problems in their life they may take a long time to get to the stage where they want to stop. I mean really want to. Like Liam they may have been dried out several times, gone to treatment centres but not actually taken personal responsibility for the whole of their life. Mainly, we do what we want to do and don't do what we don't want to do. We may say we are 'trying'. For example, 'I'm trying to lose weight' well, either I am losing weight or I'm not! That's the reality. The drinker is not accepting reality; he or she is deceiving themselves. 'I have a disease it's not my fault' is often said and yes, it is a disease, a progressive one, often fatal.

This is where, I think, the general public start to have great difficulty in having compassion for the drinker and in understanding the concept of their having a disease when he or she seemingly brought it on themselves. John G Cooney states in his excellent book Under the Weather (2002) that alcoholism is a primary, chronic disease with 'primary' meaning that as an addiction, alcoholism is not a symptom of an underlying disease state. He also describes a disease as an involuntary disability with 'involuntary' being a separate and distinct state that is not deliberately pursued. However, he says that this is not meant to suggest passivity in the recovery process and also asks us to be wary of trying to simplify what is a very complex problem.

People can get 'dried out' after which they are no longer physically dependent on ethyl alcohol but a psychological dependence remains and this needs a desire, a willingness and courage, time & effort to address, to understand and to act in a different way. There are lots of addicts that have much knowledge about their condition but if they don't change ingrained and learnt behaviour patterns there is a greater chance of relapse. Perhaps, to be 'dry' is not to drink but to be sober is not to wish to drink. And the good news is that, although the disease is progressive, recovery in sobriety is progressive too.

I can easily make sweeping generalisations on a range of subjects and with this one need to remember that no two people are alike even though they share common symptoms; that it is the addiction part that is the disease; that its effects are physical, mental, emotional and spiritual; that I cannot make a judgement as to when heavy, social drinking turns into an addiction unless I am the one doing the drinking and social drinking brings about many alcohol related problems in life too. I must remember that becoming an addict was never anyone's career choice: they didn't wilfully mean it to happen and, now, having the disease they have it for life but if they choose to they can recover. And the only way is to stop drinking completely. Insecurity, low self-worth and fear play a large part and the drinker is often emotionally immature (it is said they remain the emotional age they were when they started drinking alcoholically).

Liam told me that he spent the first fifteen years of his life more or less in permanent fear and the next fifteen drinking to stop feeling frightened. I made the classic mistake that family members often make of thinking that if the drinker has some form of counselling to establish why they first needed to drown their sorrows, to uncover deep seated, maybe unconscious, emotional causes then through understanding they can choose to stop. All the while I thought along those lines I was hindering not helping and yes, there are underlying reasons, conscious and unconscious, but the drug has taken over. Before anything can begin to be understood there has to be total abstinence. No ifs no buts.

Now we are going to stop focussing on the problem drinker because that's what most of us spend far, far too much time doing anyway. What about you and your feelings?

CHAPTER 3

The Three C's

I'm sure empathy and compassion towards your loved one are the last things you want to have at the moment. I expect you are at the end of your tether and feel emotionally drained. There must have been many promises broken, lies and so much deception that maybe you have lost all trust and are even questioning whether you like the person anymore.

Tick any of the following feelings you are experiencing:

- ☐ Resentful
- ☑ Angry
- ☑ Bitter
- ☑ Hurt
- ☑ Disappointed
- ☑ Sad
- ☑ Anxious

- ☐ Depressed
- ☐ Ashamed
- ☑ Guilty
- ☐ Disgusted
- ☐ Embarrassed
- ☑ Humiliated
- ☐ Confused
- ☑ Frustrated
- ☑ Cheated
- ☐ Despairing
- ☑ Helpless
- ☐ Frightened
- ☑ Lonely
- ☐ Self-pitying
- ☑ Self-doubting

Maybe you aren't sleeping well, always on edge not knowing what might happen next. You probably feel insecure and out of control. You may have lost your confidence thinking you are a victim and that no one else understands. These are all natural feelings to have when facing this insidious disease. But look how negative they all are. I wonder when was the last time you laughed, felt peaceful and calm, were happy; enjoyed your life? There are times when the alcoholic is contrite, makes those promises, thinks of you and perhaps gives you a gift or says something loving and you glimpse the possibility that all will be well again; for a short while.

No wonder the nearest and dearest members of the family become depressed and isolated. To have expectations raised and then dashed plays havoc with the nervous system and we either end up shutting down or becoming more and more angry and resentful often lashing out with bitter, sarcastic words and even physical violence. I know I became very dominating, arrogant and self-righteous in my condemnation of Liam's behaviour. You say to yourself: why is this happening to me? I don't deserve this; if he or she loved me they wouldn't do it. You may also contradict yourself and say; it must be my fault somehow, something I said, things I've done; maybe I do deserve this life. It is easy then for feelings of guilt and shame to creep in. Alcoholics Anonymous calls the all too familiar circular thought processes 'stinking thinking'.

How hard it is to admit a loved one's drinking has crossed over into an addiction and we can spend as much time denying the situation as they do. When the drinker refuses to accept or acknowledge they have a problem it is because the implication is that then they will have to do something about it and for them, drinking has become the only way they can cope with life. Because alcohol affects their thinking, in their confusion they equate drinking with actual survival. Our compulsion is in striving to find a solution to the problem by any means and most of us are loath to give that up. If being a member of Alcoholics Anonymous is one way for drinkers to find sobriety, then one source of help for us can be Al-Anon. Al-Anon is an organisation which provides support and enables families and friends to recover from being addicted to the addict. We have to start to focus on ourselves not the drinker and become aware of exactly what we do, through ignorance and misguided good intentions that actually prolongs the chaos and turmoil in our lives. With regard to this disease Al-Anon literature talks about the three 'Cs':

You can't CONTROL someone else's drinking pattern

You don't CAUSE someone else to drink

You can't CURE someone else's drinking problem

When I first read these sentences I understood them intellectually but I didn't believe them, if you see what I mean. All I could say was 'Yes, but'. I couldn't let go of the conviction that I had some power over what Liam did or didn't do. I know I didn't cause his addiction but there were times when I wondered if I had goaded him into taking a drink. And definitely, linked with his blindness, I did reckon I could make a difference to his emotional state and therefore whether he gave up or not. The following simple reality would not penetrate my brain:

I can't stop anyone from drinking if that is what they want to do.

The fact is that we are powerless over anything someone else chooses to do, say or think. We may be able to influence them, negatively or positively, but ultimately they actively choose. I probably did goad Liam but he chose to pick up the drink. Anyone can give me advice or make suggestions but I decide whether I take it up. To let go of trying to be caretaker and controller of another's life, I still find incredibly difficult. I have never minded my own business! My behaviour has been toned down but I continue to slip up on a regular basis. The thing is, no way do I want advice or suggestions rammed down my throat uninvited and when it happens I realise with chagrin how others might interpret my doing the same.

Here's some of the stuff I did to try and solve the madness of living with Liam:

- Searched for hidden bottles and when I found them, poured the contents away
- Peered into pubs and surreptitiously followed him down the street (admittedly fairly easy with his lack of vision!)
- Silently sniffed a lot for signs of alcohol on his breath especially when we were in the car
- Told him what to wear, asked if he'd brushed his teeth, had a bath etc
- Kept attempting to get him to eat particularly cajoling him into having some sort of breakfast
- Organised his finances and paid his bills even visiting the bailiff's office when they threatened to go to his mother's house
- When he did work I ferried him there, complete with lunch box and picked him up at the end of the day
- Tried to find any form of employment for him and racked my brains as to any other outside interest for him to do, gathered all the information and filled in forms
- Complained about everything I did and everything he didn't do plus everything he did do but carried on in just the same way

- Drank with him so he would leave with me and stopped drinking when we decided on periods of abstinence; persuaded him to try controlled drinking and then monitored him keeping a diary
- Telephoned around and went out to search for him when he was missing
- Locked the doors afraid of him coming back unexpectedly
- Literally left the country to get away for a break
- Gave ultimatums telling him he had to leave and reneged on them every time
- Cleared up after him and I don't mean when he spilt something
- Had violent fantasies of wielding a scimitar and slicing his head off!
- Made excuses for him, which I genuinely believed, in front of other people and his relatives
- Blamed his family for not understanding (who understood only too well) and the barmen who carried on serving him
- Got upset saying he didn't care about me and was selfish; if he loved me he would make an effort to stop
- And ultimately, denied that alcohol was the real problem

Maybe some of these are familiar to you? Is this a sane way to behave? I felt as if I was looking after a rebellious teenager but, look at me, I was the over-protective, critical parent! It was an obsession. As well as all that there was the crying, the trying to reason with him, the treading on eggshells, the silent treatment, the trying to please, the hiding from him, the hiding money from him, the waiting on him, the consoling when he felt sorry for himself and the rest. After yet another 'last straw 'as I have already told you, I did call the police once but I was lucky Liam wasn't violent towards me and he doesn't drive, thank goodness. He got himself into trouble and out of trouble with the law; I wasn't involved. Nor did I use sex as a weapon by refusing to sleep with him or acquiescing to undesired intercourse, nor did I cheat on him.

Let's face it, it's not normal behaviour and shows in stark reality that no-one can manage that kind of life indefinitely without becoming ill. Anyway it didn't make a blind bit of difference (pardon the pun). You can think all the thoughts feel all the feelings and do all the actions but nothing will make a difference. None of the above solved the problem which is why I repeat: you cannot stop anyone from drinking. And so what can you do?

CHAPTER 4

Detachment

You can change. You deserve to have a life filled with dignity. You have power over your own life. As they say 'life is not a rehearsal' so don't you want to enjoy it, laugh and be light-hearted, feel free, achieve your ambitions, realise your dreams even if they are different ones than you thought they might be?

You can start to change your attitude. I expect you're saying: why should I? Well, when I say there is a lot you can do whether the alcoholic is still actively drinking or not, I never said it was easy or that you would like it! It's like the chicken and egg conundrum—if you change your behaviour towards the drinker your attitudes will change and if you change your attitude you will find your behaviour has started to change. Yes, it's a risk; there may be no change in the alcoholic's behaviour. Taking a risk is a leap of faith but others' experience has taught that in this situation if we do risk changing our ways then family life is bound to improve.

There are several things you can start by not doing. One step at a time, when you are aware of the following, try one or two, see what happens and note how you feel whilst also trying to remember all the time that your loved one doesn't want to live like this either despite all they may say:

- Don't search for hidden bottles (I know, very difficult)
- Don't monitor how much they drink (it will always be more than you think)
- Don't pour it away (they will always get more and in ways you won't have thought of in a million years)
- Try not to treat the alcoholic like a child (you wouldn't if it was someone you didn't know)
- Try not to criticise, reproach or nag (if you get what you're after it will only be a pyrrhic victory)
- Try not to start an argument or get hooked into one when they are under the influence of alcohol (they may be all too physically present but really they are emotionally absent and so it's a waste of breath. Our breath is life, we cannot afford to waste it)

A word about the 'if you loved me you wouldn't do x, y or z' syndrome. He or she probably does love you but they need and want alcohol more. That is the fact of the matter and what's more they most likely feel ashamed and guilty most of the time, more than you can ever imagine which in turn propels them into trying to find solace in drinking. For instance, you wouldn't say 'if you loved me, you wouldn't have cancer or you wouldn't have Alzheimer's or you wouldn't be obese'. No one person can fulfil all your wants, needs, desires. If you start to feel and act like a victim your self-confidence, perhaps innately low, will go downhill and if you are asking the alcoholic to be responsible for themselves and their behaviour then you have to be responsible too. Besides, being narky, offhand, contemptuous or whiny is not a good look!

Two tenets of Al-Anon are:

Don't threaten unless you are prepared to carry out your threat

Don't create a crisis but don't prevent a crisis if it is the natural course of events

If you go back on a threat it's a bit similar to a small child demanding a packet of crisps; you keep saying no but eventually say yes–not good practice if it becomes a pattern as the child never knows where the boundaries are and will, naturally, begin to not believe you resulting in manipulating behaviour and gradually, as they get older, they may start to resent you as may the drinker even though it can be their actions that have brought the situation about. Because this is an uncomfortable feeling they may suppress it resulting in behaviour that is passive-aggressive. But then it could be said that by becoming dependent on drink, becoming incapable and irresponsible is a way of getting rid of a deep felt anger.

Not preventing a crisis takes a hell of a lot of courage because it goes so much against the grain not to help in some way. Again with children, as I'm sure any mother will recognise, it takes supreme effort to let them experiment when there may be even a small element of harm that could befall them and even 18 year olds off to college can have parents fraught with anxiety.

Somehow, we must resist doing things for the drinker that they can do for themselves and not only them but for anyone else too. The problem belongs to us; we are protective because of our own fear. People change from a point of pain; we learn from our own mistakes. We have to steel ourselves from jumping in to save the drinker because a crisis can be a necessary stepping stone to recovery. We read about the alcoholic needing to reach rock bottom before they completely desire a different way of life but perhaps the same applies to ourselves.

Caring *for* someone infantilises them, caring *about* them does not. When you can gradually make the shift from 'for' to 'about' you are starting to detach. In fact, you are doing something momentous; you are cultivating the art of detachment. It is a skill that we all need in our lives and to practise it not just with our loved ones. Put simply it is minding our own business. Then again, probably many of you have started not to care at all!

I remember beginning to detach from Liam with utter indifference I was so frustrated and angry with him, overwhelmed and ill that I began to care less and less what he did and when he did it. The last time the ambulance crew carted him off, asking if I was coming along too I told them in no uncertain terms—no, I was not! But it is detachment with compassion, detachment with love that I am asking for here; it is the letting go of someone and allowing them to have their own thoughts, feel their own feelings including pain and choose their own actions. Now, I'm sure a lot of you can be habitual people-pleasers and so detaching can seem as if you are rejecting the person with the alcohol problem which means, in all likelihood, you will sabotage your efforts since it feels too uncomfortable.

Please be aware of this possibility. This characteristic of people-pleasing is rooted firmly in our upbringing; we have learnt this way of being to get the results we want. I admit that I have always felt the need to make sure everyone around me is okay before I can relax and please myself. The tape playing in my head says to me: if you make yourself needed (by any means available) then you will be liked, loved and wanted and therefore you will not be alone/lonely/abandoned. Because most people have difficulty coping with ambivalent feelings and attempt to get rid of the positive or the negative at any one time, we often vacillate between indifference and making threats to needing to rescue, prevent the crisis and calm any situation.

Yes, detaching with compassion can benefit the alcoholic but it is you that I want to reap the benefit. I don't want you to suffer because of them or allow yourselves to be manipulated, abused or deceived but you have become part of the problem and have been drawn into a game-playing scenario which you cannot win. Understanding that the drinker is ill, knowing the facts, facing reality and moving the focus onto yourself will protect you, improve your well-being and happiness whether the other person continues to drink or not. I promise.

From this chapter the phrases to contemplate are:

MYOB: Mind Your Own Business

Detachment starts with respect for someone's individuality, seeing that person as separate, different and whole and worthy of existing in any way they choose

CHAPTER 5

Plan B

If detachment is a skill, it has to be practised and like all skills improves over time; with neglect it can become rusty but once learnt is never quite forgotten. And detachment, especially with compassion, is a life time task for co-dependents. Melody Beattie in her informative book Codependent No More (1992) states: 'A co-dependent person is one who has let another person's behaviour affect him or her, and who is obsessed with controlling that person's behaviour'. I say again, I suspect that you were inclined to be co-dependent long before the present problem arose (it may well have been that one or both of your parents were or are problem drinkers) and as old habits die hard, please don't get disheartened if you manage to detach one minute but not the next or have a good day followed by a week where it's the same old story. We are human and one of the major hindrances is that we are also likely to be perfectionists.

Another major factor in the quest for detachment with love is the alcoholic who probably won't like this change in you one little bit. Be prepared for a backlash in their behaviour where things can seem to get even worse for a while. That's why it is so important for you to take steps to avoid the usual triggers to protect yourself and not get drawn into familiar patterns of behaviour. What I am talking about here could be described as: hindsight, mid-sight & foresight. We all know that magical place called hindsight but here the point is to recognise a potentially difficult area while you are in it and to do something to stop the situation getting worse. This is mid-sight. Ideally, you get to the stage where you see trouble brewing and refuse to engage at all: foresight.

A personal trick that helped me with Liam and continues to help in everyday life when my buttons are pressed is imagining a luxurious purple velvet cushion, visualizing holding it in front of my tummy and creating a metaphorical distance between me and the other person. I find this useful when on the telephone too. Thinking now, it stands to reason that it should be placed in front of the solar plexus area (a complex of radiating nerves at the pit of the stomach); the place where our 'gut' feelings come from because it's the uncomfortable, anxious feelings I want to ward off. Another visual imagining might be a powerful, protective, golden-coloured cloak hanging from a tree that I pluck off and swirl around my shoulders so that no-one can reach me or invade my space. You can make up your own to help give you enough distance. Discover that you don't have to react to provocation or be hurt by cruel words, be forced to do anything you don't want to do or make any decision you are unsure about.

Of course, you can actually leave the room before your equilibrium is lost or end a conversation on seeing where it might be heading. You take responsibility for your part in any interaction: you can choose to remember that the other person is ill; that your well-being doesn't depend on anything they say, do or feel. Frequently, I got in the car and drove away just because Liam couldn't and yes, I went as far as taking the ferry to England! I was going for other reasons anyway but knowing I was literally unable to sort out any crisis or pick up any pieces, so to speak, and that someone else would have to deal with his antics was a huge relief.

This is where Plan B comes in. Or C or D, E & F, if necessary! Don't forget all this is designed to help you feel better and get your life back. Anyone who lives with and/or loves a problem drinker knows that the best laid plans can evaporate and usually just when you are convinced that this time all will work out okay. There were parties and gatherings we didn't get to because Liam was missing or so drunk he couldn't stand up and also those I vehemently wish we'd never managed to get to. I still cringe at the memory of a football dinner & dance where I was so embarrassed to be with him. I had dithered about accepting the tickets, intuitively knowing it was a bad decision yet still hoping I was mistaken. If only I had known what I know now: hindsight, eh?!

And so, it pays, along with foresight, to have a little forethought. Perhaps you can have a spare set of car keys, house keys and some money set aside somewhere, enough say for a B&B, if you feel the need to leave in a hurry. This sounds rather dramatic but if the drinker becomes aggressive or violent then your responsibility is to keep yourself safe and your children safe. It might be a good idea to agree with a neighbour or friend that they will look after the kids on the spur of the moment if needs be—I know, you don't like to ask! In lesser cases, to save going to a social gathering alone or not going at all, talk to your friends explaining the likely scenario and ask if anyone would like to come with you at short notice whether to the theatre, concert, or birthday party etc. You may be surprised at how keen they are to have a night out themselves.

There are many activities you can do on your own too. I enjoy going to the cinema alone for instance. What were your hobbies and interests? I say 'were' as they may have lapsed since you have been all consumed with the alcoholic. Brief, necessary exits can be going for a walk, taking a bus ride, going to a cafe with a magazine for example; anything to break the habitual pattern of action/reaction.

You don't have to accept unacceptable behaviour. Possibly, you think that in order not to accept it you have to stay and fight it and make sure your loved one knows it is unacceptable and that what I am suggesting is fleeing it and therefore, in some way condoning the behaviour. Plan B opens up your choices when faced with a particular reality and like an army you can surrender but you don't have to submit. Surrendering is giving up fighting, letting go, while submission is more like lying down and possibly being trampled on. You can give up struggling without losing your sense of self and individuality. The power is with you and you choose what you are going to do about any situation. Plan B is about having something or someone on your side to prevent yourself being drawn into the futile battle with alcohol.

We cannot avoid frequently feeling disappointed, resentful and often despairing but by thinking of a Plan B we are acknowledging reality whether we choose to put it into place or not. I am reminded of a Zen proverb:

"If you understand, things are just as they are;
if you do not understand, things are just as they
are."

Try substituting the word 'accept' for 'understand'. To accept a reality and not try to change it constitutes freedom not oppression.

CHAPTER 6

Yes, But...

If you are still saying 'yes, I know, but...' go back to the beginning and start again!

I'm only half joking because we can't go forward to find a fulfilling life outside our predicament if we don't grasp these fundamental lessons first. Of course, that's not to say there is one definitive eureka moment but more a gradual understanding, a subtle realisation and a shift in our way of being. Perhaps now is a good time to recap and realise just how much of a shift may have already occurred:

Your family member or friend is ill not a bad person.
They crave a drug which is addictive.
This addiction is probably 10% physical and 90% psychological.

Although no-one forces them to put the glass to their lips or swallow the liquid, they never meant their lives to go down this route.

Anyone can become addicted; if you drink enough for long enough even you.

Most people deny they have a problem.

Denial has many sides, layers and levels to it.

Maybe you deny you have a problem too.

The drinker has a disease, a disease that is progressive.

You and the whole family are affected by it.

An alcoholic suffers physically, emotionally and spiritually.

Their family suffers physically, emotionally and spiritually.

The drinker can recover but only if they stop drinking.

You can recover whether they stop drinking or not.

You are powerless over the drug that is alcohol.

You cannot change anyone except yourself.

The drinker has a right to be responsible for his or her actions.

More than likely, if you take on the role of caretaker or rescuer of another human you will soon want to persecute them and when they defend themselves you will end up feeling like a victim.

Focus on your own life to enable you to start to detach.

It helps to have alternative practical plans in place to avoid repeating old patterns of behaviour.

When you detach with compassion, understanding and forgiveness there is a much greater chance that the problem drinker will take steps towards their own recovery.

A friend of many years was in the same boat with her daughter who often phoned at all hours in a crisis situation whereupon my friend would drop everything to sort out the problem: whether rushing to the hospital or salvaging the car after an accident or listening whilst she sobbed, under the influence, about lost jobs and friends; even to the point of taking over her daughter's finances, arranging bills to be paid, rationing money for entertainment, buying extra food and petrol, not to mention any medical prescriptions together with the cost of therapy. Her daughter carried on as normal while my friend couldn't sleep at night though she had turned her mobile phone off and stopped answering the landline or the door bell. How her friends contacted her I don't know!

The daughter is a lovely natured girl but whenever I listened to the stories I felt she was still a teenager. Actually, she is 35 years old and could easily have a teenager herself. My friend felt guilty most of the time; she felt it was her fault as a mother because of various upheavals in the past and was always frightened that if she didn't step in her daughter might really hurt herself. Interestingly, her other daughter travels around the world independently solving whatever problems arise with barely an input from her mother. My friend's feelings of responsibility were exacerbated because the three of them had bought an investment apartment in which the 'needy' daughter lived and any mortgage shortfall would still have to be paid if she couldn't cover her rent.

I use the past tense because my friend has had the courage to change a lot of her behaviour when she understood it was her feelings of fear and guilt preventing her daughter from metaphorically leaving home and taking charge of herself come what may. When she acknowledged reality and faced up to possible accidents and unwanted financial loss (because her plan B became to sell the apartment if necessary) she was able to acknowledge some suppressed resentment and disappointment, quite possibly linked to her own mother. Consequently, the daughter had to take responsibility for her actions and now she is living a stable, enjoyable life with a solid boyfriend at her side, though my friend has to be constantly on her guard not to slip back into her own old familiar caretaking ways.

And to my shame I find myself still interfering in Liam's life and his achievements since, although there is no longer the drink, there is always the lack of eyesight. Much of the time I have the best of intentions but taking on any responsibility that belongs to him robs him of the chance to feel good about accomplishing anything, however small. When I manage to detach with love I am offering support by freeing him to experience a range of feelings from satisfaction and joy to disappointment and frustration.

There is a conundrum: how can you trust someone if they are not trustworthy but how can they be trustworthy if they are not trusted. Trust is a leap of faith. Live and let live. It's hard to 'let live' when you have got into the habit of picking up the pieces, been focussing on damage limitation for so long and probably all but forgotten how to 'live'. Now you have started let's go on to look at ways you can gain more peace and serenity, lessen your anxieties and experience joy.

CHAPTER 7

Mindfulness, Meditation and the Meaning of Life

Practising detaching is so alien a behaviour for us that for a while your anxiety will no doubt increase. It certainly did for me and my friend confirms that not intervening and letting whatever was going to occur actually happen meant her worry levels rocketed. Luckily, she has a variety of hobbies one of which is the intricate painting of ceramics that demands all of her attention in the doing of it and herein lays the key: staying in the present moment. It's tricky staying in the present unless we are busy working or being entertained—when we are 'doing', but when we are just 'being' is usually when unwanted thoughts enter. In fact many of us can't stop 'doing' for fear of what may happen as if the act of being busy somehow wards off bad things.

If we were brought up in households where one or both parents drank excessively then staying comfortably in today, in the moment, is hard. We can seek to create drama, tension or excitement, even if unpleasant, as we have become used to it and hooked on it subconsciously. Being in the moment, in reality, even if it is okay can seem dull or boring and so we can go into our heads feeling the need to bring in thoughts and remembered times from the past with all those slights and hurts. We re-open conversations; re-feel things, recreating the scenes and mixing it all up with what's going on today. Then we begin to fantasize about the future determining how it will pan out usually with negative anticipation. Spiralling out of control away from now, we are lost. Everyone does this so don't tell me you don't!

The mantra of Alcoholics Anonymous is: one day at a time. If a drinker, once dried out, can manage not to have alcohol for one day, or one hour at a time or even one minute at a time if that is what it takes then the minutes, the hours and the days add up to the weeks, months and years. It is the same for us as family and friends of problem drinkers. We are changing habits of a lifetime and by taking very small steps, one day at a time, we learn that by being consciously aware of staying in the present moment and not letting our thoughts wander off, worry, anxiety and fear are banished. Broken up into small parcels of time life becomes not only bearable but precious.

Thich Nhat Hanh, the Buddhist monk, calls this mindfulness and in his book The Miracle of Mindfulness (1991) describes it as 'keeping one's consciousness alive to the present reality' (page 11). He teaches that when paying attention becomes a habit it not only restores a sense of calm but means we are 'alert and ready to handle ably and intelligently any situation which may arise' (page 14). In a nutshell, if you are washing up but thinking of the cup of tea you will have afterwards you are not actually washing up and probably, while drinking the tea you are compiling a mental list for the afternoon's trip to the shops perhaps not even really aware of holding the cup. You are 'sucked away into the future.... incapable of actually living one minute of life' (page 5).

Probably you do have to be a monk to practise mindfulness all the time but it is amazing what happens when we remember to do it. When practised properly it's impossible to be anxious; if worrying thoughts do enter it proves we've lost the attention. I've noticed an improvement in my memory and a feeling of relaxation because of the knowledge that if whatever it is, is not happening right now I'll worry about it, whatever it is, when it does and crucially, if it does. This is the crux of many of our problems: most anxiety or fear is fantasy.

When what you are anxious about isn't happening now then it doesn't exist so why worry until it does? If it does the situation is very unlikely to be exactly as you had imagined it which means you can never rely on your 'fantasy' reaction. You will always be forced to react to something in the present moment that it happens, in other words, more spontaneously and by definition not in a planned way. And so, there is no point in wasting the present moment fearing something that will be different anyway if.....!

'If' is the word I want banished from the dictionary–notice how I have used it in the last paragraph. 'If' belongs to the future or the past:

If 'x' hadn't happened then we wouldn't have....

If 'y' goes ahead then 'z' should be.....

If I could.... then I would.....

If he didn't want.... then he should have.....

Grammatically these examples are in a conditional tense i.e. not definite; i.e. fantastical!

> *"Worry never robs tomorrow of its sorrow; but only saps today of its strength"*
>
> A.J.Cronin

What did you miss while you were preoccupied, away in your head having conversations? Did the sun come out and you never noticed? Was that a bird singing that you never heard? Just looking out of the window is a very good way of bringing the focus back to reality since however dull the view there is always something going on: some movement to concentrate on, a different way to look at the same things; the way the light falls or a change in colour. Another thing is to listen to outside sounds, to be aware of their different distances and, of course, there is people-watching which is guaranteed to bring you back and keep you in the present as long as you don't start imagining that their lives are better than yours! In other words it is the act of observing which automatically brings the focus back to the outside world.

My favourite trick for being in the here and now is to listen to myself breathing in and out, not so much the noise but the action of breathing. When I do this I can't think about anything else and it's easy to do anywhere: e.g. sitting on the bus, watching TV, walking along, whilst ironing! It's very calming and actually a form of meditation. I always thought to meditate properly I had to be sitting cross-legged, bolt upright, chanting something and if I wasn't I couldn't be doing it properly. Purely personally, meditation to me is achieving an awareness of now, being still and with an openness to receive whatever may arise without feeling fearful, with a lack of expectation where I can inhabit the space around me. This can be managed in the quiet of the countryside or a bustling city scene. Being internal and external at the same time, I suppose—it's a work in progress as they say. After all, the dictionary says that to meditate is to contemplate and that contemplation is to survey in the mind, think deeply or view thoughtfully meaning there isn't much to get wrong about it.

All I know is that it is crucial to make the time to stop doing and just be, on your own, for at least half an hour every day. Your time to sit and read, listen to music, snooze or power nap, stare into space, knit or whatever takes your fancy; no arguments, half an hour is possible for anyone. We make time for what we want to do and so, if you say you haven't the time then I say you don't want to. And if you find you can sit with your eyes closed and breathe deeply, in and out through your nose counting each complete breath for, say, ten times, when you open your eyes you will feel refreshed and restored. Or you could light a candle and gaze at it; most of us have been entranced and comforted by the flickering of an open fire at some time or other. Alternatively, eyes closed, say over and over again silently the word 'calm' or any mantra you may have come across or play the sound of waves breaking on the beach or other relaxation music; any music that doesn't create nostalgia taking you away from the present again.

"The time you enjoy wasting is not wasted time"
Bertrand Russell

For anyone who is religious, prayer is a form of meditation and every good thought is a prayer, which brings me to spirituality and what it means. For our purpose here it has nothing to do with religion and for want of a better phrase I see spirituality as a connection to 'the bigger picture'. This is about faith and therefore risking trust, in life itself, in ourselves; letting go of control and the need for perfection, letting others live and for our part living simply, loving generously, speaking kindly, caring deeply and leaving the rest to a power greater than ourselves, however you want to interpret that.

Living with the disease of alcoholism means we often become physically ill, it certainly disturbs our mental capabilities, creates turmoil in our emotions and depletes us spiritually. When I was drowning in Liam's problems making them my own, I forgot I believed in something. I forgot about the light at the end of the tunnel. I forgot to marvel at Nature: the changing seasons, how even the smallest insect is part of the whole, the performance of the weather, the importance of the moon; the whole miracle of the Universe. I forgot to be humble and I forgot to be grateful; to be positive, focussing only on the negative side consumed with worry, anxiety and fear and completely out of balance.

Most importantly, I didn't realise that I was allowed to ask for help and I don't mean asking a person but just silently, genuinely giving out a request for help into the ether, so to speak. I'm sure most of you have uttered 'please God' many times not necessarily meaning a religious God. I am amazed at the results and if you are genuine, honest and courageous and prepared to look at your part in any interaction you will be assisted. For me there is no such thing as a coincidence which means that when you ask for help you need to pay attention and be open to what occurs, whatever form it takes. There is more happening than we can ever realise or understand. Just think of a few amazing bits we do know like dogs' sense and range of smell we cannot comprehend; the elephants inland in Asia who sensed the tsunami approaching through their feet; the cells of a caterpillar that become new cells of a butterfly; the light we see from the stars that no longer exist; the sound waves we don't hear that produce a picture of a baby in the womb; the electricity we can't see waiting for us to flick the light switch. What amazes you? I like to use the metaphor for a higher power as a TV channel that I'm not tuned into but it's available if I press a different button.

In my life every decision I have ever made has brought me to where I am now: all is connected. I have no regrets about all the stressful, soul-searching or sad times; they have taught me so much. How do we know the experience of joy unless we have known sorrow? Everything needs contrast to put it into context. Kahlil Gibran describes this spiritual concept so eloquently in his book The Prophet (1992). We don't exist in isolation we are part of the whole and I believe we have a role to play and a duty to the world to stand assuredly in our own space, to be well, to be humble, recognising that everyone else is as human as us and struggling to make sense of life too. Being grateful helps this process and here I am talking about all the small things and all that we take for granted. You might like to:

- go through the alphabet each letter being something for which you are grateful or
- think of a few things just before you go to sleep or

- write down a list, put it away, then come back to it at a time when you are feeling particularly stressed

Number one for me when I think of Liam is how so fortunate I am that I can see; it doesn't get more basic than that. I can gaze at the stars, he has never seen one. Feeling grateful improves my mood too which improves my self-esteem, as well as instilling hope, encouraging me to remember that things can just as equally turnout well as badly.

When I feel confident I can afford to be generous towards others and treat them with the respect they deserve. I say 'afford' because this is about value and worth: a sufficient level of self-confidence means you are always in a safe, secure place and can practise giving and receiving rather than taking and I mean true giving rather than giving to get. Feeling resentful, victim-like and mealy-mouthed we project horrible outcomes and how things will affect us negatively, never positively and worrying won't ever protect us from the future but only prevents the vitality of being in the here and now, of living today, of appreciating all the small stuff and viewing our surroundings in awe. The more self-confident we become the more we can trust by understanding at a deep level that no one can hurt the spark, the light, the spirit, the still small voice, the soul inside; however you want to describe that part of you that exists beyond the physical body.

> *"If the only prayer you said in your whole life was, 'thank you' that would suffice."*
>
> Meister Eckhart

CHAPTER 8

Press Pause

Let's pause and take stock again before moving on. I wonder if you can see where I am going with this, what I have been attempting here?

When we get overwhelmed with the apparent needs of others and are consumed with the desire to help and fix everything since it seems they can't or won't take care of themselves, it is useful if we can remember that a higher power exists for others too. It can help to visualise handing them over, for example, like holding a bird in your cupped hands, opening them and allowing it to fly away, free; or a ball of sunlight encasing them, going wherever they go, being with them always. I really have to practise what I preach as Liam is loath to use a white cane and I can become quite anxious thinking of him in unfamiliar places. When I manage to hand him over I find I am free to enjoy myself and be my top priority.

From, at the beginning, feeling stressed out, at the end of your tether, totally obsessed with what the problem drinker was or was not doing, saying, thinking or feeling and so turned in on yourself, racking your brains for a solution to a problem that doesn't belong to you—more later on the one that does—you have gradually expanded outwards back into the outside world:

- **you have learnt the facts about the drug alcohol and how it affects the body, mind and spirit**
- **you have accepted reality**
- **you know you did not cause, you cannot control or cure another's drinking habits**
- **you are practising detachment and are allowing the other person to be responsible for their actions and their thoughts and their feelings**
- **as this is extremely difficult, you have a plan B in place to help you mind your own business and keep you safe**
- **you stop yourself being anxious or fearful by staying in the present**
- **you spend some time everyday relaxing or resting to revive your energy and sense of self**
- **you have started to be grateful for what you do have partly by acknowledging the people, places and things we all take for granted**
- **you are open to the 'bigger picture' and understand you can ask for help**

- **you begin to trust that assistance will arrive even in the most unlikely places and strangest of ways**
- **hope comes back into your life and you come to believe in the possibility that life can unfold in a good way**

"Life, for all its agonies of despair and loss and guilt, is exciting and beautiful, amusing and artful and endearing, full of liking and love, at times a poem and a high adventure, at times noble and at times very gay; and whatever (if anything) is to come after it—we shall not have this life again."

Rose Macaulay

And so, now you don't have to be CEO of the World anymore, you can have some fun! I want you to get out and about. You are your top priority. Over time our feelings and desires have been devalued and our creative ideas and thoughts have been dismissed, mainly by ourselves. A feeling of unworthiness creeps in destroying our vitality and imagination in an almost imperceptible and subtle way. I know it's hard not to feel guilty when someone else is probably feeling fed up, frustrated or depressed and to let them be and go out and enjoy your life. It's difficult to have a good day when someone you care about is struggling but you have to save yourself. Here I'm not talking about the half an hour's relaxation time; that's just essential for energy, nor am I referring to Plan B because that's just a back up to stop you falling into the trap of arguing with a drunk or staying in the victim role. No, this is about enjoyment, pleasure, excitement, joy—remember those?

Of course I don't know anything about your circumstances: you probably work, you may have small children or not so small ones; maybe it's your child you are concerned about or a parent. Neither do I know what extra-curricular activities you can afford or commitments you have already but I do know how vital it is to expand your environment. I expect many of you had hobbies or interests that have been abandoned that perhaps you can start up again? Outside activities especially where you can meet new people will enhance your frame of mind and you will feel better all-round. There are lots of free things you can do, exhibitions you can see or groups you can join; anything to get your creative juices going. Is there anything you have always wanted to have a go at? A word of warning here—many get involved in voluntary work and find it helps them gain a different perspective on their own lives, however, as my guess is many of you are innate caretakers, it may not be such a good idea to begin with to go from the frying pan into the fire.

Several years ago I had a go at something I didn't know I was interested in. I volunteered to help out backstage with the local amateur dramatic society; scenery, props, costumes that sort of thing but they cast me in one of the main parts—help! It turned out to be brilliant fun and such a boost for my self-esteem to confirm that not only could I learn lines (I'd always wondered how stage actors managed it) but could deliver them too and conquer the fear of being in the spotlight. I've been involved every year since, quite the old pro! It just shows that you never know what's round the corner.

Lightening up is so important but at the same time you might consider getting some outside help in the form of counselling. This is because we must face up to the fact that all of us enabled the drinker to go on drinking even though we may be unwilling to admit it. It is necessary to delve into why and what it is about you as an individual that encouraged you to do so; seeking assistance from a third party who is unbiased is far better than friends or family who always have their own agenda. Many treatment centres run courses for 'concerned persons' as they tend to call us. Low cost counselling is available if needs be. There are contact details for a number of agencies in the appendix at the back; also, as I have already mentioned Al-Anon exists to help friends and families of alcoholics.

I know it takes courage to confront the more shadowy side of the self but how can we ask the drinker to change the habit of a lifetime unless we are prepared to as well? A lot of our behaviour is unacceptable too when we don't realise it; it's as ingrained as theirs. Now we shall go on to look at one of the main reasons why.

"Experience is not what happens to you, it's what you do with what happens to you."
Aldous Huxley

CHAPTER 9

Expectations

Someone said that expectations are resentments under construction. We think our loved ones let us down but really it is our expectations that let us down, not them and this is all about the 'mind reader effect' as I call it. All my expectations about anything or anyone or any situation are silently based on all of the experiences so far in my life. I say 'silently' since most of them were formed during my childhood, many outside of memory and, this is most important, many, many are expectations that I don't realise I have. Most of the time, I'm not even aware that I expect others to read my mind; I just become disappointed and resentful when whatever I didn't know I was hoping for doesn't happen.

We have hopes and expectations of all our relationships based on how we grew up, witnessing how others behaved especially our parents. What we saw them do, heard them say and how they said it, the opinions they expressed and all the prejudices they held, all the assumptions they made, every nuance of body language became the normality of our world. Added to all this is the strata of society we were born into, how much or little wealth the family had, what constituted the extended family and their location as well as the accepted culture of the time. There are a myriad of unconscious influences that form our often unconscious expectations and again, I haven't even mentioned religion or politics! Common expectations exist but yours are unique, even your brothers and sisters have their own differing views since they were born at a different time, treated in a different way although maybe seemingly the same; a different take on normal. I'm sure you get the idea.

No one person can meet all our expectations even if we were able to be aware of the exact detail of them at any one time and so we certainly cannot expect someone with a drink problem, under the influence of a drug, to meet any expectation we have of them. Look at the double expectation you have just read! It's a minefield and no wonder we end up seething with resentment and deflated through disappointment time after time.

When the expectations I didn't know I had aren't met, depending on how important they are, I usually become defensive and then react inappropriately which in turn can often mean I experience feelings of shame or guilt afterwards; either that or I stay angry, sullen and down. Then it's easy to blame the other person (or the weather or the government or the dog!) the result being the erosion of the relationship. This happens to everyone but I wonder what you do when what you are hoping for doesn't work out? Can you see a pattern?

I want to observe what I do and understand why I do it so that I can change things and feel more content, calm and peaceful but first I need to know actually what it is that I really want. I need to know as I have to tell people because I can't think of anybody I know who has a crystal ball. I believe that these hopes and dreams belong to the five year old inside the adult and the vast majority are unrealistic (most probably because they are based on the desire for unwavering, unconditional love). Combine these unexpressed, unrealistic expectations with alcohol and there's a major problem brewing.

Every time you feel hurt is really a hope that hasn't been fulfilled; an expectation that hasn't been met. It isn't the other person's actions at fault, just the mismatch between your inner world and the outer reality. There is no point in saying 'don't expect anything' as the pictures in this inner world of imagining of how we want life to be will always exist. However, lowering our expectations is prudent, so then we can allow ourselves to be pleasantly surprised.

Once, I and a group of acquaintances were invited to a mutual friend's wedding in Cape Town. I was grateful to be invited not knowing her very well but really I didn't mind whether I went or not, not having a burning desire, at the time, to visit South Africa and so, consequently hadn't built up an idea of how I wanted it to pan out. The ten day trip was one of the best I've experienced; even at the time I realised it was largely due to not having pre-conceived hopes. The problem is you can't manufacture this attitude.

I think what you can do is practise catching hold of your expectations, examine their origin then ask yourselves: is it realistic or even fair to expect this now? Externalising them like this makes it easier to actually tell the other person what you want. Even the simplest wishes have to be spelt out otherwise how does anyone know? The irony is, when the little person inside you acknowledges the hopes and dreams, makes them a little more achievable and asks someone to fulfil them, there is a much greater chance of the original coming true.

> *"If you have built castles in the air, your work need not be lost; that is where they should be. Now put foundations under them."*
> Henry David Thoreau

It's not so easy when dealing with a loved one's alcohol addiction. Here our expectations need to be so low they can only go higher! First there may have to be a period of mourning, and I mean to put it this dramatically, because there can be a great sadness akin to grief when we finally realise that what was so hoped for is never going to happen. The person addicted to the drug may never be able to provide the companionship and love you desire in the case of a spouse, partner, girlfriend/ boyfriend or have a bright future complete with family life if this person is your son or daughter or be the special friend and confidante you may want your sibling to be. When one or both of your parents are the alcoholics, the sadness is not dissimilar to the loss felt when a parent dies: the opportunity is lost forever of their being the perfect parent you always longed for even though, as adults, you know intellectually that perfection is not possible.

Realising that even reasonable expectations are not going to be fulfilled often brings a second wave of resentment and anger towards the drinker together with a frustration of being put in this situation resulting in self-pity and feeling like a victim. Think of the word resentment: from the Latin *sentire* to feel; we are feeling again (re-feeling) something from the past. No wonder it's so easy to go into victim-mode and isn't all resentment just self-pity? Not only that, but resentment is so acidic and toxic (like the alcohol!); I always find feeling resentful plays havoc physically with my digestive system.

Go ahead process all the feelings, don't attempt to damp them down as the fire will only start up again, then find other people and places to get some of your needs met whilst looking inside yourself to meet most of them. It may come to the point, having explained and expressed yourself clearly, where you find it necessary to weigh up whether you can go on existing in this present way or need to work towards an alternative way of living with or without the drinker.

Of course, whatever happens, we are left with our expectations of ourselves where we tend to set the bar unusually high or far too low. Whether your self-esteem has always been low or living with active drinking has diminished it, my guess is you boost it by caretaking others, and by extension controlling them, at the same time self-flagellating by feeling not good enough or that you haven't achieved perfection or at least not done something well enough (been able to stop the drinking being a case in point). You are always working to sort stuff out, achieve, organise so that then and only then will you be able to let go and relax. Only when you are exhausted, burnt out and frayed at the edges do you stop. Oh, silly me, you are there already!

Hand in hand with these over optimistic goals comes the dismissing of the real talents you possess. Isn't it true that one major character shortcoming is often denying the existence of our positive qualities? We take care of others and want to make others happy perhaps at the expense of our own prosperity all the time seeing this as a virtue when really it is the opposite. Maybe some of the traits you ignore are your true assets.

Can you list 10 positive qualities you have/things you are good at:

1.
2.
3.
4.
5.
6.
7.
8.
9.
10.

Was that quite difficult? Ask a friend to fill it in about you, really taking on board what they say. In fact ask several friends independently because what they come up with will help increase your self-respect and with a good level of self-respect

- you will be better able to set good boundaries;
- better able to continuously do what you say you are going to do;
- less likely to try to force others to change;

- start to recognise your limits;
- cease destroying your self-respect by having guilty feelings

"He that respects himself is safe from others; he wears a coat of mail that none can pierce."
Henry Wadsworth Longfellow

Living with someone who abuses alcohol, we often lose sight of all the good in us and in the drinker. We become polarised either stepping onto the pedestal looking down on all their shortcomings or impersonating servants forgetting our abilities and achievements. Lowering expectations means less hurt, less resentment, less self-pity and from that position it's much easier to forgive both the drinker and ourselves. Being aware of unrealistic wishes is another useful reality check regarding our powerlessness over alcohol.

Our own expectations are probably unrealistic; our expectations of the alcoholic definitely are.

Just before we give up on expectations; a cautionary word about your hope of recovery and expectation of a stress-free existence. I'm sure you'll be able to manage all that I've been urging in time. And time is precisely what it takes. There will be days of clarity and times when you feel you haven't progressed at all. Please don't expect too much too soon. Take one step at a time—progress not perfection. I'm asking you to turn 360 degrees from obsessing about another to keeping the focus on yourselves—always. It's the task of a lifetime to change the habit of a lifetime but, believe me it's worth it as you are worth it. It works. Every time you turn the focus onto yourself and examine your behaviour and what you can do to change, you give the person with the alcohol problem an opportunity to change too. It is extremely powerful.

Now I shall talk a little about sobriety and living with someone who is not actively drinking since this naturally brings its own set of expectations.

CHAPTER 10

Sobriety

With Liam it took me five years to let go. To let go of thinking I was more important than him, better than him, right when he was wrong, good when he was bad, a model citizen when he was an arsehole, a layabout, a good for nothing; five years to stop being inexcusably arrogant. I judged him, criticised him, punished him all the while telling him all the things he should, ought to, must do yet carried on doing everything myself with very bad grace. By detaching and leaving him to it I showed I cared. It sounds perverse but by staying, coping and being a martyr in effect, I was exercising pity and indicating Liam was a failure and had no hope of going it alone or of recovering. Apparently, the concerned person focuses on what the alcoholic says and not what he or she does but the alcoholic doesn't hear what we say only heeding what we do. I finally married my actions to my words.

Often the desire to stop drinking occurs after a particular crisis brings a realisation, extra acute remorse during a hangover or perhaps following a prolonged period of despair and hopelessness. At this time I cannot overstate how important it is for the drinker's family and friends to support him or her but not to force the issue. Since you are now armed with knowledge about alcoholism and your attitude is wiser you are well placed to really assist. There is no need to even use the word 'alcoholic' just acknowledgement of a drinking problem is enough. It is useful to have informed yourselves about A.A. (Alcoholics Anonymous) either by phone, leaflets or attending an open meeting as well as having a chat with your doctor for other forms of help available BUT it is up to the drinker to get the help they need in whatever form they want. Of course, there is a temptation to rush in, organise and sort out as soon as possible in case they change their minds. PLEASE DON'T–that's the same motivation as before isn't it? Don't be over-protective.

I've no idea exactly what happened to Liam and how he got sober; he doesn't really remember himself. In my mind it's no coincidence that my making the decision to let him live whatever life he chose gave him the impetus to stop drinking for good. He denies this but I know, definitively, it was the catalyst. In hindsight I think his stays in the psychiatric hospital and the treatment centres were part of a process: the gradual discarding of each vestige of denial for Liam and for me. It's my hope in writing this that for you it may be easier but every drinker has their own set of difficulties and I'm afraid it may take more than one attempt before sobriety is gained. Try not to despair. Hope need never be abandoned and by doing all I have suggested you will gain recovery yourself and help the drinker more than you know. When they make it sobriety really is reincarnation in the same lifetime.

There is a wealth of information on what the drinker can expect from sobriety but, again, here I want to focus on what it may be like for you. Liam attributes his new life beginning to the first day he rang and asked me if he could come round for coffee and talk as that he does remember. Although I kept him at arm's length for quite a while I sensed all was very different this time. I owed him support as I was just as much a part of the whole problem and gradually we spent more and more time together. Since it's like getting to know someone all over again many adjustments must be made. There is the so-called 'pink cloud', I suppose like a honeymoon period, when one looks through rose-tinted specs and yes, in the beginning there was such relief and renewed hope and yes, expectations but after a while I began to realise that more or less I was feeling the same anxieties as before though obviously toned down.

One day when in town I noticed I still glanced in every pub I passed to see if he was in there and once, later on, when I saw him in the street outside an hotel, anxiety fluttered in my stomach. He had admitted that sometimes when we were at his place in the city he'd tell me he was going out for a cigarette only to dash across the road to the hotel to down a double vodka the barman had ready for him and be back indoors within normal fag time and since I now knew this, of course, I wondered if he'd just come out of the hotel and had 'slipped'. A.A. says that a 'slip' or relapse is when a sober alcoholic has a drink or gets drunk again and here I'm not talking about coming out of a treatment centre and going for one straight away on the way home. There are many reasons why this can happen (many never have a relapse–as far as I know Liam hasn't) and easily because the drinker has forgotten what being an alcoholic means. As they recover their health and their lives become more manageable, resembling normality again, it can be simple to suppose they could have a drink in an ordinary social setting and all would be well. For friends and family this can set us right back bringing up the old feelings of hopelessness and fear. It's often a one-off, not necessarily repeated, and so perhaps it could be seen as helpful since everyone may become over-confident and unrealistic about what can be achieved and how quickly. Basically, anyone can forget to live one day at a time.

Liam was sober but I slipped constantly as I totally forgot that I was as powerless over his sobriety as I was over his drinking. I'd read about cross-addictions (when one addiction is halted then others can come to the fore as with gambling, sex, recreational or prescription drugs) and have to admit to half-filling the instant coffee jar with de-caffeinated coffee after monitoring Liam's vastly increased intake! And, worrying about HALT–recovering alcoholics are told to be wary of becoming hungry, angry, lonely or tired as this puts them under unnecessary stress and could prompt a 'slip'–I was forever buying sweets and putting them in his pockets like he was a child. The main source of anxiety was my need to keep the peace not only between Liam and myself but also when we were out and about mixing with other people. My fear was that if I or anyone said or did anything controversial it might start a row then Liam's levels of frustration and anger would increase and he'd deal with it by having a drink as he had always done in the past.

Also there was the booze question: should there be alcohol in the house and what about when I wanted to have a drink or when friends came round? You have to do what feels right for you plus whatever is comfortable for your loved one; talk about it. For a couple of years at least I decided not to have any in the house and definitely not to drink when in Liam's company but, again, this was largely because of my own fear. Liam, I think, was ambivalent: he was grateful but also irritated that I couldn't act normally. Seven years on and sometimes there is a bottle of wine in the cupboard, I have a drink when we eat regularly at the local where we met and now don't worry when and if we entertain or visit friends. Come to think of it, for a long time, he's had a boxed bottle of whiskey tucked away waiting to go as a raffle prize; it bothers me from time to time when I think of it whilst he never gives it a thought!

It wasn't that I was so naive to think everything would be hunky-dory but finding myself still monitoring, scrutinizing, watching, snooping, caring for and on, if not red, amber alert because fear continued to be my default setting, I was confronted again with my own behavioural problems, though less severe, and the realisation that I had brought them into the relationship; Liam's drinking had only exacerbated them.

In hindsight I wasn't very patient with myself though I was conscious of being patient with Liam as well as respectful, courteous and appreciative of his efforts and courage every day. I minded my manners. What became more and more wonderful as time progressed was being able to talk to him and explain my feelings of nervousness around alcohol, my worries for his welfare and for the future and receive an understanding response. I remembered not to bring up the past or blame him, although I desperately wanted answers and details of certain events to complete the jigsaw, to make sense of the previous five years and prove without a doubt I hadn't been mad. I still don't know the half of it but by now it's ceased to matter.

Whether your family member chooses to recover through A.A. or some other way you can expect them to become, let me say, slightly obsessive. Needing healthy displacement activities they may focus on a variety of hobbies or interests in short bursts of enthusiasm or prolonged dedication. Liam did all sorts of courses, learnt to water-ski, went off trekking for charities to far flung parts of the world, fishing with his mates, weekends away and all the time building up a network of new acquaintances and contacts. I've heard of some in recovery becoming fanatical about their health, having a fetish about fitness or getting into extreme sports in a big way.

It seemed to me if Liam wasn't asleep (newly recovered alcoholics are often very tired for a year or more) or on the phone, he was out doing something or other or helping fellow problem drinkers. He still wasn't around! Once again resentment can surface and this time jealousy can come with it; try to be encouraging and focus on your own friends and interests. Each day without alcohol is a miracle. People talk about the 'isms' meaning if you take away the alcohol there is still the 'ism'. The person in recovery isn't a different person they still have all the emotional difficulties that caused them to go down the road to addiction and all the defensive behaviours. If you were secretly hoping for a magic wand it can be deflating but life calms down and balances out eventually.

Detachment is still vital. There will be setbacks but all of us learn from mistakes; talk them through and then forget them. Communicating and understanding each other's feelings is the key.

And so, in sobriety we need to remember:

- the illness took a long time to develop and recovery is a slow process too
- every recovering alcoholic needs to learn how to manage in a world where alcohol remains freely available
- not to be over-protective
- we are responsible for our own fear and anxieties
- if we want someone to be trustworthy, we have to trust them
- to be patient and tolerant
- not to play the blame game or bring up the past
- to guard against feelings of resentment and jealousy
- if we want to feel heard and understood we have to communicate in a cordial, constructive and candid way
- ambivalent emotions and defensive behaviour are a part of normal life
- to continue to focus on ourselves
- whatever happens is better than the drinking days

CHAPTER 11

Sex

For those of you whose husband, wife or partner is in recovery, a word about sex. As far as I am concerned sexual intimacy with an actively drinking alcoholic is as oxymoron! Alcoholism aside, although we may be able to perform the act of intercourse, many couples find achieving sexual intimacy very challenging. For a start, it depends on how we were brought up to experience our sexual selves plus a myriad of outside influences bringing their pressure to bear on the intimate relationship between two people. We tend not to like discussing sexual difficulties in public and privately there's really no one to talk to either unless we go down the route of a trip to the sex therapist. Even with the full-on media coverage in the 21st century of all things sexual, this is usually a step too far; only for others, not us, and you can't trust friends not to gild the lily!

I think the major difficulty in achieving a mutually satisfying intimacy for most is the dilemma, we as humans face, of ambivalence. I want to love and desire the person I also sometimes don't like. How much can I trust this person with my inner self? How vulnerable can I allow myself to be? How close can I get to this other and still remain a separate self? How can I find the balance between dependence and independence? We need a separate volume on how to achieve a fulfilling sexual intimacy without adding a drug into the mix.

Each relationship tends to find its own compromise but a sexually intimate relationship with an active problem drinker is likely to be miserable, unfulfilling, deeply frustrating and downright depressing. The actual sexual act may be satisfactory but I doubt it somehow whichever sex is the drinker. There will be different difficulties for men with alcoholic wives or girlfriends than for women though the loneliness, hurt and feelings of being unloved are the same. Added to these, for women there will probably be the man's erectile problems and many complain of hygiene issues leading to revulsion and a loathing for the other as well, perhaps, for the self for having allowed their bodies to be misused. All of us can have sex we don't want in order to keep the peace and not have the sex we do want to punish the drinker. How can we feel nurtured, held and understood at the deepest level when our partner is emotionally and mentally absent? Alcohol kills a mutually loving sexual relationship.

Sobriety certainly brings about the possibility of repairing the damage over time. Equally, it can highlight the gap in intimacy created during the drinking years or the avoidance of intimacy that was always there in the relationship but camouflaged by alcohol. To begin with it's like getting to know a stranger all over again, both people perhaps feeling quite bashful, with the over-riding feature of this time being the amount of guilt the recovering drinker probably feels. This means they may avoid intimacy at all costs, refusing even to talk about the subject. Added to this, perhaps they had brief affairs or one night stands under the influence and are left feeling wretched especially if the details are more than hazy. Of course, you may have had some yourself, striving to find the love that was lacking.

Sometimes the reason why the relationship started in the first place can be the key to sexual problems. As has been said previously, alcoholics are usually emotionally dependent personalities due to their experiences in childhood leading them towards addiction in the first place but also leading them to unconsciously choose partners (in the case of men) who will care for them and act out the mother role. This mother/child type of relationship is hardly conducive to a healthy, mature sex life. Put on a pedestal of perfection the woman is felt to be unapproachable, even angelic. Strength and goodness are projected on to her whilst the man feels he remains unworthy; a mere flawed mortal. This can be accentuated if she has stood by him through to sobriety. Half knowing this he may hate the situation and want to punish her but be too afraid to act for fear of losing her. Consequently, for him avoidance of intimacy may be the only way out and the couple's sex life may not recover.

However, it takes two to tango and the woman, as carer, probably has an equal reticence about sexual intimacy hiding behind this role, despite protestations to the contrary, because of her own background. All need not be lost. Like any other relationship problem it needs to be explored and understood before action can be taken. The relationship exists as an entity in its own right, a bit like a bank account, thriving on what is put in by the couple and depleted by withdrawals. A problem or unhappiness for one person is a problem for the relationship and needs to be discussed and solved by the couple together.

With my being older and Liam's eyesight meaning he always needs some practical help we can still fall into the mother/child role now he's sober, one that I admit was prevalent during the drinking years and, yes, was 'the fit' that drew us together in the first place. Concerning intimate relationships, psychologists seem to imply women search for a replica of their father and men their mother: the unconditional love and perfection that is the fantasy of the ideal parent of the opposite sex. What they stress less is the likelihood of our also seeking out and ending up with someone who possesses the more negative qualities too, even if we strive to avoid this at all costs.

All I know is that in Liam I have ended up with my father without meaning to. Not to do with the drinking problem but more concerned with what was behind that coping mechanism for both of them. Yes, Liam was courageous hauling himself into a better life having that inner strength though now I am left with someone who is equally reticent (my dad would hide behind the paper or a book, his attention to me span upsettingly short) and who, not on purpose, keeps his thoughts and feelings locked up. It's frustrating and often a little upsetting as it promotes a feeling in me of being rejected. No wonder though, growing up in an alcoholic home he was silently told: don't talk; don't feel; don't trust. I am reminded of an article on communication–it is my responsibility to communicate with someone not theirs–if I don't feel I am being understood or heard it only means I need to express myself in an alternative way and continue to do so until I get what I want. And that presumes I know what I really, truly want when it comes to loving, nurturing and cherishing.

I don't deny intimacy is a tricky area for me and for Liam. Maybe we have reached a point where the relationship is good enough but dissatisfactory for both of us. It must be 'good enough' if neither of us does anything to change it. For my part I realise I've probably successfully been avoiding sexual intimacy throughout my life. Maturing at the beginning of the psychedelic seventies in the era of sexual freedom for women, with the Pill freely available, I thought I was really emancipated and that my varied sexual experience equated with intimacy but, no, experience just kept my vulnerability at arm's length–a cover up! Looking back I can see all my sexually intimate relationships including my marriage were with men who were unavailable for one reason or another: 'three week wonders', already married, living in another country, over fond of mind altering drugs or who just kept their distance because of their own difficulties. Of course, the bottom line was that I didn't feel worthy of being loved or being found attractive. I find it ironic that I had to get to the older and wiser stage in life, which naturally brings some loss of libido and where a frequent sex life is not so important anymore, for me to realise this debilitating fact and to exorcise the ghost of the shy, uncertain woman that was my mother's daughter and to feel assured in my sexuality.

Often there's a longing for something that passes through me resulting in a bit of self pity, probably only the fantasy of an ideal love or maybe just regret for the missed opportunities of the past. It doesn't last long and reality brings me back to the understanding that if I want to receive affection from Liam and feel loved, cherished and appreciated, I have to give affection and appreciation; I can be the one to love and cherish remembering there are many different forms of intimacy. I can hug or kiss him first; I can focus on all the ways he does show he cares about me and not what is lacking. He is no more the expert than I am and so let it begin with me; let me be the first one to take the risk; to risk possible rejection. After all, the fear of rejection and the deep anxiety that we may be un-loveable makes us all act defensively, hanging back waiting for the other person to make the first move, to be the first to expose their feelings.

"All the beautiful sentiments in the world weigh less than a single lovely action"

James Russell Lowell

CHAPTER 12

Serenity

What is serenity exactly? For some it may materialise as a swan silently gliding through the water, posture erect, floating unperturbed through life but for others this vision can seem too calm, too torpid. They need activity, friction, a dynamic to propel them to creativity and wish for sound and movement and change to feel good. The dictionary defines serenity as tranquillity. For me it is the inner tranquillity achieved from living without emotional fear; a tall order for most and especially for anyone living with the disease of alcoholism. How can we attain this state? All that I have been talking about throughout this book are the little steps that move us towards that place of inner peace.

I shall tell you how I manage it (of course I don't an awful lot of the time I'm only human) and I shall be striving to maintain the quality of serenity for the rest of my journey through life. However, I find I can be both peaceful and calm yet dynamic, passionate, creative and involved in the moment because I know there is a position inside myself where it exists that I can access, not necessarily immediately but without too much hard work, anxiety or battle with the 'self', by understanding the mental moves required and the practice I need to exercise.

- I seem to accept myself now, warts and all, meaning I like myself better without so many conditions needing to be in place before I deem my actions acceptable and worthy of approval. The inner critical parent is not seeking perfection to the same extent. Perhaps this is a natural consequence of the ageing process but also a direct result of being better able to

- Accept others as separate from myself and allow them to lead their own lives in the way in which they choose even though I may not approve and without the burning desire to change them which means

- Being able to sit with ambivalent feelings and not project the uncomfortable ones outside of myself onto someone or something else which

- Lessens the need to react defensively due to anxious or fearful feelings and when I am not defensive I feel an okay person with no need to be afraid. Each time I don't react in a defensive manner makes it easier not to do so the next time someone 'presses a button' so that when I am wrong I can

- Say sorry sooner, knowing criticism can be a pointer to help me be aware of my shortcomings enabling me to
- Detach and not be so easily offended by the words and actions of others who are doing the best they can at any one time most likely not meaning to hurt me anymore than I do them. When there is offence it is probably
- My expectation of a situation that doesn't match the reality. Recognising this I can let go more easily asking myself how important is it really which immediately lessens resentment and therefore, self-pity and without self-pity I am
- Able to solve problems logically rather than emotionally. My life is manageable: what seems urgent is not necessarily important and there is always time enough for what is truly important keeping in mind the knowledge that as
- All difficulties pass I can afford to be patient so that when I am tempted to worry about the future I can
- Bring my focus back to today stopping the internal conversations and concentrating on the outside world which leads to
- Gratitude for all that I have rather than what I lack, actively practising having positive thoughts which always bring small, unexpected joys reinforcing my belief that
- Nothing is a coincidence, I am not alone; there is a power greater than myself and all manner of stuff

going on way beyond my senses or comprehension.

I can live without fear.

Like I say, no way do I manage all of this all of the time, only some of it some of the time. The key point is now I know when I experience serenity and when I don't and, of course, there are days when I don't manage any of it any of the time! I like the definition of 'slip' I hear that A.A. uses: serenity losing its power.

Serenity is really the ultimate acceptance of personal responsibility: letting go of our disappointment that the world can't conform to our desired model of it, the realisation that the buck stops each, every, all the time with each one of us never allowing us to project unwittingly onto others, giving us power over ourselves, our actions and reactions. Nobody is responsible for us and we are responsible for no other adult (excepting those with special needs). It can be a lonely place and sometimes a burden but mostly really and truly liberating.

In an ideal world I should like to see you as relatives and friends of problem drinkers support them emotionally whether they have the courage to stop drinking or not and whether or not you make the decision to remain living with them. We don't have to accept unacceptable behaviour from anyone and that means not accepting it from ourselves either. We are all struggling human beings trying to make sense of the world and doing the best we can at any one time. By keeping the focus on ourselves we can better see what options are available to us, what changes we can make rather than only seeing what changes we think others need to make. We don't have to wait to solve a problem.

Be honest. See alcoholism for the disease that it is, detach with compassion, make a life for yourself, build up your self-worth so that you need less defence mechanisms, practise personal responsibility by looking at your part in any interaction and you will be rewarded with a feeling of serenity and peace.

"Nothing can bring you peace but yourself."
Ralph Waldo Emerson

EPILOGUE

'Our very life depends on everything's recurring
'til we answer from within'
Robert Frost

Was my father an alcoholic? I still don't know and the question is not mine to answer anyway. He alone could have said yes or no and that would have depended on his ability to face reality. I am left with the fact that what he drank and the amount he drank affected his physical body and I suspect throughout the time I knew him he was beleaguered emotionally and spiritually. He drank because it was part of the culture and of his job and then probably because he was depressed. Or maybe he was depressed because he drank, or both. He was an emotionally dependent man and boy, certainly physically dependent on pain killers, probably sleeping pills and a host of other medication mostly prescribed to counteract the side effects of one another. Alcohol was his drug of choice to ease him through the slough of despond.

I am as I am through exposure as a child to the conscious and unconscious behaviour of my parents, our place in society, the agenda of the time and age in which I grew up and the knowledge prevalent in the wider world. This is as it remains for everyone. It doesn't really matter if Dad had a drink problem as long as I use my past experience to inform the present in order to become aware of how I behave, take risks to change my ingrained habits and grow in spirit. In that way and only through that process can I encourage, assist or help others. That's genuine help not manipulation. When I remember to mind my own business without giving advice unless it is requested and let other people feel their own pain, experience their own thoughts and live their own lives, how, when and where they choose as only they can do, then I consciously feel happier, less stressed, calmer and more content. Crucially, when I concentrate on my own life, of which I have way less than half left, I definitely feel more confident in the company of others and my self-esteem stays at a level where I have no need to be defensive. I can afford to be genuine.

This encompasses what I am asking you to do too, no ifs no buts. Experiment with one small change every day and just note what happens. Sometimes experiments work and sometimes not but each time they are conducted brings you more understanding if you pay attention. Please try it. To do so is not selfish, nor self-centred, it is self-respect. Ultimately, you are all you have and, on all levels, please look after yourself. Care about others not for them. I agree it is hard work. The much quoted prayer by Reinhold Niebuhr which has become somewhat of a cliché is really all we need. You can take God out of it if it means you feel more comfortable and more likely to try it. Here it is:

God, grant me the serenity
To accept the things I cannot change;
Courage to change the things I can;
And wisdom to know the difference

I wouldn't change any part of my life. The difficulties and the sorrow are hard to bear at the time but 'wow' what a lot have I learnt and am learning daily. I am so grateful to Liam for being blind and drunk since his experience, my experience and our experience together is teaching me so much. If he had just been blind drunk I think I may well have passed him by. There is much that works between us and a lot that doesn't but, hey, a bonus, he can't see my wrinkles! He loves me for the woman I am not how I appear and, by embracing sobriety, has become the man I always thought he was which in turn helps me to repair the unconscious, repressed parts of my relationship with my father who, in his lifetime, was unable to help himself. It would be rude to ask for any more. Undoubtedly, there will be other hurdles ahead but anything given to us is manageable if life is lived one day at a time, one moment at a time, NOW.

"Do what you can, with what you have, where you are."

Theodore Roosevelt

APPENDIX I

Where alcohol takes its toll

Whilst binge drinking at the weekend isn't a brilliant idea, if these 'weekenders' abstain from drinking during the week they at least give their internal organs a chance to recover (such as the liver, the pancreas and the kidneys) and it may be the constant drinkers: glass of wine (or two!) on return from work, to relax or with a meal that do more damage since their bodies never have a recuperation period. Let's state again now that half a bottle of most wines today contains 5.25 units. And again, hopefully stating the obvious, the body finds it more difficult to cope with the drug ethanol the older it becomes. Exact guidelines may vary as do different people's reactions but John G Cooney (*Under the Weather*, 2002) says that for men 22-50 units per week and for women 15-35 units per week is hazardous drinking.

Some of the effects, starting in the head and working down:

- From the outset; mood swings, aggression, irrational behaviour, arguments, nervousness, chronic anxiety, unknown fears, depression. Low blood sugar reduces concentration and memory. Unsteadiness and double vision (vitamin B1 deficiency)
- Alcohol is a diuretic and so there may be permanent dehydration causing dry skin and low energy levels. Facial deterioration, puffy eyes, signs of ageing (especially in women), dilated blood vessels giving a flushed look, perhaps eczema and psoriasis
- Ultimately, blackouts (alcohol amnesia), hallucinations, seizures (especially with abrupt withdrawal), epilepsy, damage to nerves, serious psychiatric disorders, dementia (wet brain)
- Mouth cancer, throat cancer (cancer of the larynx), cancer of the oesophagus, chronic coughing
- Trembling hands, tingling fingers, loss of sensation and numbness (peripheral neuritis), excessively red palms of hands with sweating, thinning of arms (body less able to make lean muscle tissue)
- More prone to colds & flu, reduced resistance to infection (reduced white blood cell count), increased risk of pneumonia and tuberculosis
- Anaemia, impaired blood clotting, high blood pressure, breathlessness, weakness of heart muscle, heart failure

- Weight gain, particularly around the belly, obesity-related diseases
- Vitamin deficiency, gastritis/irritation of stomach lining/heartburn as excessive juices flow back to oesophagus. Ulcers. Vomiting, diarrhoea and eventually malnutrition. Stomach cancer
- Inflammation of the pancreas (low abdominal pain that used to subside after a few days) becomes acute
- Diabetes
- Duodenal ulcer
- Pancreatic cancer
- Fatty deposits build up in the liver over time (without any effects being felt for some years), alcoholic hepatitis can develop where liver becomes temporarily inflamed (dull ache on right side with flu-like symptoms), jaundice, cirrhosis of the liver (liver cells replaced by scar tissue preventing liver from functioning properly–ceasing alcohol intake altogether can stop cirrhosis getting worse but liver failure may have already set in)
- Liver cancer
- Impaired kidney function, urinal infections
- Reduced fertility in both sexes. In men: impotence, testes can atrophy and male breasts can develop as liver damage blocks the body's ability to produce male sex hormones. In women: unwanted pregnancies, risk of giving birth to deformed/low birth weight/learning disabled babies

- Impaired sensation/numbness in legs can lead to falls, skin damage can make wounds slow to heal, ulceration, tingling toes, peripheral neuritis, gout (build up of uric acid crystals) in joints of big toes

This is by no means an exhaustive list! Tolerance to ethyl alcohol goes up over time but then declines. Signs of alcohol dependency are finding it difficult to cut down followed by withdrawal symptoms such as shaking, feeling nauseous which are alleviated by having a drink. Undoubtedly, the harmful consumption of alcohol creates social, legal, domestic, job and financial problems. If heavy drinking is continuous and as a person gets older the effects of ethyl alcohol on the body become irreversible, lifespan may be cut by ten to fifteen years whilst added to all this is the risk of death through accident or suicide.

- **1 unit equals the amount drunk (ml) multiplied by the strength of the drink (ABV %) divided by 1000**
  (www.nhs.uk/livewell/alcohol)

APPENDIX II

Useful Agencies & Organisations

You can find information and ways to find help through the following websites:

www.alcoholicsanonymous.ie 00353 (0)1 842 0700) – there are open meetings you can attend to help you understand what it is like for the alcoholic

www.alcoholics-anonymous.org.uk 0044 (0)845 769 7555

www.al-anon-ireland.org 00353 (0)1873 2699 for families and friends of alcoholics

www.al-anonuk.org.uk 0044 (0)207 7403 0888

www.nacoa.org.uk 0044 (0)800 358 3456 (free from UK) confidential helpline for children of alcoholics

www.alcoholireland.ie

www.alcoholresponse.com

www.thehanlycentre.com 00353 (0)1 280 9795

www.rutlandcentre.ie 00353 (0)1 494 6358

www.cuanmhuire.ie 00353 (0)59 8631493

www.stpatrickshosp.com 00353 (0)1 249 3200

www.nhs.uk/livewell/alcohol

There are numerous agencies offering counselling & psychotherapy but, personally, I think it is important to obtain a referral to someone specialising in alcohol addiction.

APPENDIX III

Bibliography & some other books in which I have found understanding, solace & optimism

Alcoholics Anonymous, (2003), *Big Book, Fourth Edition,* A.A. World Services Inc, New York

Al-Anon Family Groups UK & Eire, *World Conference Approved Literature*

Beattie, M (1987), *Codependent No More,* Hazelden

Berne, E (1968), *Games People Play,* Penguin

Botton, A de (2000), *The Consolations of Philosophy,* Penguin Group, London

Chopra, D (2003), *SynchroDestiny,* Rider

Chopra, D (2004), *The Book of Secrets*, Rider

Chopra, D (2000), *How to know God*, Rider

Cooney, J. G (2002), *Under the Weather: Coping with Alcohol Abuse and Alcoholism*, New Leaf

Garner, L (2004), *Everything I've Ever Done That Worked*, Hay House

Gibran, K (1992), *The Prophet*, Penguin

Giono, J (1989), *The Man Who Planted Trees*, Peter Owen Publishers

Hagen, S (1999), *Buddhism plain and simple*, Penguin

Hanh, Thich Nhat (1991), *The Miracle of Mindfulness*, Rider

Harris, T.A (1973), *I'm OK – You're OK*, Pan Books Ltd

Jeffers, S (1991), *Feel the fear and do it anyway*, Cornerstone

Jung, C.G (1986), *The Undiscovered Self*, Routledge & Kegan Paul

Kabat-Zinn, J (2012), *Wherever You Go, There You Are Mindfulness Meditation for Everyday Life*, Piatkus

Scott Peck, M (1990), *The Road Less Travelled*, Arrow

Skynner, R/Cleese, J (1991), *Families and how to survive them*, Mandarin

Smith, M.J (1975), *When I Say No, I Feel Guilty*, Bantam

Redfield, J (1994), *The Celestine Prophecy*, Bantam

Rice Drews, T (1980), *Getting Them Sober Volume 1*, Bridge Publishing, USA

Rice Drews, T (2002), *Getting them Sober Volume 2*, Bridge-Logos USA

Rice Drews, T (1986), *Getting Them Sober Volume 3*, Bridge Publishing USA

Rice Drews, T (1992), *Getting Them Sober Volume 4 Separation Decisions*, Recovery Communications Inc

ABOUT THE AUTHOR

Originally from Marlow, Buckinghamshire in England, Anne trained and worked as a couple-counsellor with Relate for a number of years after running her own businesses in the retail sector. For the past twelve years, Anne has been living and working in Ireland where she met her partner.

Also by the author: *Has it all gone pear-shaped?* How to build better relationships by understanding why they can go wrong, Morshead A/Munro J (2000), Veritas ISBN 1-85390-546-1

CPSIA information can be obtained at www.ICGtesting.com
Printed in the USA
LVOW13s1603240713

344448LV00005B/590/P